CHRISTMAS

The Annual of Christmas Literature and Art

CHRISTMAS

CHRISTMAS

The Annual of Christmas Literature and Art

VOLUME SIXTY-TWO

AUGSBURG FORTRESS, MINNEAPOLIS

In this volume

Leafing through this year's volume of CHRISTMAS, one might notice a subtle British aroma rising from the pages. We owe much in our celebration of Christmas to our cousins across the Atlantic. A bit of their contribution to the season is sampled here.

Caroling, for example, is a popular English tradition that has given rise to much Christmas music. Breaking with our own tradition in this book, we begin with "The Christmas Story" in the form of a service of lessons and carols. Modeled after the service made famous by the King's College Choir of Cambridge, England, the service relates in scripture and song the story of our redemption from the fall in the Garden to the manger in Bethlehem. The music selected is suitable to small gatherings so that you can have your own home celebration. Peter Church, himself a native of England, provided both the cover illustrations and the initials that dot the pages of this section.

A twist on another British music tradition is presented in the article "The Boys Choir of Harlem," which traces the phenomenal growth and success of this young singing group.

Then for a real taste of Britain, brew yourself a pot of tea and try the recipes found in "A Christmas Tea" on pages 50-55.

The English artist and social reformer William Morris, father of the Arts and Crafts Movement, is recognized in the article titled "The Adoration," which also features his ornate tapestry of the wise men's visit to the baby Jesus.

For fiction lovers, this volume offers five new short stories. Each story illuminates a different human response to the arrival of Jesus on earth.

Selected poems and clever illustrations, including "The Twelve Days of Christmas" as fancifully portrayed by Dave LaFleur, complete this literary as well as visual feast of holiday fare. We hope you enjoy it all.

—THE EDITORS

Table of Contents

Editorial Staff: Gloria E. Bengtson, Jennifer Huber, Lois D. Johnson.

Book Design: Koechel Peterson & Associates, Inc.

THE CHRISTMAS STORY
A Service of Lessons and Carols
~
Once in Royal David's City

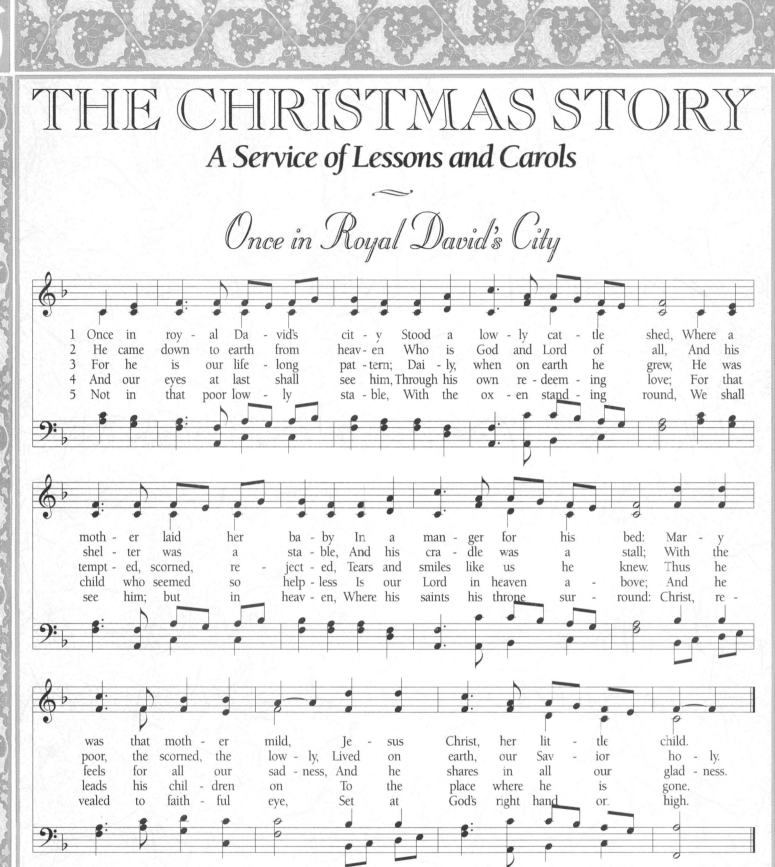

1 Once in roy - al Da - vid's cit - y Stood a low - ly cat - tle shed, Where a
2 He came down to earth from heav - en Who is God and Lord of all, And his
3 For he is our life - long pat - tern; Dai - ly, when on earth he grew, He was
4 And our eyes at last shall see him, Through his own re - deem - ing love; For that
5 Not in that poor low - ly sta - ble, With the ox - en stand - ing round, We shall

moth - er laid her ba - by In a man - ger for his bed: Mar - y
shel - ter was a sta - ble, And his cra - dle was a stall; With the
tempt - ed, scorned, re - ject - ed, Tears and smiles like us he knew. Thus he
child who seemed so help - less Is our Lord in heaven a - bove; And he
see him; but in heav - en, Where his saints his throne sur - round: Christ, re -

was that moth - er mild, Je - sus Christ, her lit - tle child.
poor, the scorned, the low - ly, Lived on earth, our Sav - ior ho - ly.
feels for all our sad - ness, And he shares in all our glad - ness.
leads his chil - dren on To the place where he is gone.
vealed to faith - ful eye, Set at God's right hand or. high.

Words: Cecil Frances Alexander, alt.   Music: melody Henry John Gauntlett; harmony Arthur Henry Mann

The family or assembly may gather around a piano or may sit at a table or around a room and sing without accompaniment. A circular or semicircular arrangement, good for singing and viewing the book, is desirable. Those gathered may sit or stand, or stand only for the opening and closing hymns, whatever seems best for the occasion.

CAROL: "Once in Royal David's City"

BIDDING PRAYER
A parent or grandparent or other respected member of the group who reads well begins with this invitation and prayer.

Beloved in Christ, at this Christmastide let it be our care and delight to hear again the message of the angels and in heart and mind to go to Bethlehem and see this thing which is come to pass, the babe lying in a manger.

Therefore, let us read and mark in Holy Scripture the tale of the loving purposes of God from the first days of our disobedience to the glorious redemption brought us by this holy child.

But first, let us pray for the needs of the whole world; for peace on earth and good will among all people; for unity in the church he came to build and, especially, in this our community.

Let us remember the poor and helpless; the cold, the hungry, and the oppressed; the sick and them that mourn; the lonely and the unloved; the aged and the little children; all those who know not the Lord Jesus or who love him not or who by sin have grieved his heart of love.

Lastly, let us remember before God all those who rejoice with us, but upon another shore and in a greater light, that multitude which no one can number, whose hope was in the Word made flesh and with whom in the Lord Jesus we are one forevermore.

These prayers and praises let us humbly offer up to the throne of heaven, in the words which Christ himself has taught us:

Our Father, who art in heaven,
hallowed be thy name,
thy kingdom come,
thy will be done,
on earth as it is in heaven.

Give us this day our daily bread;
and forgive us our trespasses,
as we forgive those
who trespass against us;
and lead us not into temptation,
but deliver us from evil.
For thine is the kingdom,
and the power, and the glory,
forever and ever. Amen

CAROL: "I Am So Glad Each Christmas Eve"

I Am So Glad Each Christmas Eve

1 I am so glad each Christ - mas Eve, The night of Je - sus' birth!
2 The lit - tle child in Beth - le - hem, He was a king in - deed!
3 He dwells a - gain in heav - en's realm, The Son of God to - day;
4 I am so glad each Christ - mas Eve! His prais - es then I sing;

Then like the sun the star shone forth, And an - gels sang on earth.
For he came down from heav'n a - bove To help a world in need.
And still he loves his lit - tle ones And hears them when they pray.
He o - pens now for ev - 'ry child The pal - ace of the king.

Words: Marie Wexelsen; tr. Peter A. Sveeggen, Copyright © Augsburg Publishing House.

Music: Peter Knudsen

Different people may take turns reading the lessons.

THE FIRST LESSON: Genesis 3:8-15
God tells sinful Adam and Eve that they have lost the life of Paradise and that their seed will bruise the serpent's head.

THEY HEARD THE SOUND OF THE LORD GOD WALKING IN THE GARDEN IN THE COOL OF THE DAY, AND ADAM AND HIS WIFE HID THEMSELVES FROM THE PRESENCE OF THE LORD GOD AMONG THE TREES OF THE GARDEN. THEN THE LORD GOD CALLED TO ADAM AND SAID TO HIM, "WHERE ARE YOU?"

SO HE SAID, "I HEARD YOUR VOICE IN THE GARDEN, AND I WAS AFRAID BECAUSE I WAS NAKED; AND I HID MYSELF."

And He said, "Who told you that you were naked? Have you eaten from the tree of which I commanded you that you should not eat?"

Then the man said, "The woman whom You gave to be with me, she gave me of the tree, and I ate."

And the Lord God said to the woman, "What is this you have done?" And the woman said, "The serpent deceived me, and I ate."

So the Lord God said to the serpent:

"Because you have done this,
You are cursed more than all cattle,
And more than every beast of the field;
On your belly you shall go,
And you shall eat dust
All the days of your life.
And I will put enmity
Between you and the woman,
And between your seed and her Seed;
He shall bruise your head,
And you shall bruise His heel."

CAROL: "Sussex Carol"

Sussex Carol

(unison)

1 On Christ-mas night all Christ-ians sing, To hear the news the an - gels bring, On
2 Then why should we on earth be so sad, Since our Re-deem-er made us glad, Then
3 When sin de-parts be - fore his grace, Then life and health come in its place, When
4 All out of dark-ness we have light, Which made the an - gels sing this night: All

Christ - mas night all Christ - ians sing, To hear the news the an - gels bring,
why should we on earth be so sad, Since our Re - deem - er made us glad;
sin de - parts be - fore his grace, Then life and health come in its place;
out of dark - ness we have light, Which made the an - gels sing this night:

News of great joy, news of great mirth, News of our mer - ci - ful King's birth.
When from our sin he set us free. All for to gain our li - ber - ty?
An - gels and saints with joy may sing, All for to see the new - born King.
"Glo - ry to God and peace to men, Now and for e - ver-more. A - men."

Words and music: Traditional English

THE SECOND LESSON: Genesis 12:1-4a

God promises to faithful Abram that in his seed all the nations of the earth will be blessed.

HE LORD HAD SAID TO ABRAM: "GET OUT OF YOUR COUNTRY, FROM YOUR KINDRED AND FROM YOUR FATHER'S HOUSE, TO A LAND THAT I WILL SHOW YOU.

I will make you a great nation;
I will bless you
And make your name great;
And you shall be a blessing.
I will bless those who bless you,
And I will curse him who curses you;
And in you all the families of the earth shall be blessed."

So Abram departed as the Lord had spoken to him.

CAROL: "I Saw Three Ships"

A soloist may sing the story; everyone may join in at the refrain, "On Christmas Day . . . ."

I Saw Three Ships

1 I saw three ships come sail-ing in,
2 And what was in those ships all three? *On Christ-mas Day, on Christ-mas Day,*
3 Our Sa-vior Christ and his la-dy.

I saw three ships come sail-ing in,
And what was in those ships all three? *On Christ-mas Day in the morn-ing.*
Our Sa-vior Christ and his la-dy.

Words and music: Traditional English

4 Pray, whither sailed those ships all three?

5 O, they sailed into Bethlehem.

6 And all the bells on earth shall ring,

7 And all the angels in heaven shall sing,

8 And all the souls on earth shall sing.

9 Then let us all rejoice amain!

THE THIRD LESSON: Isaiah 9:2,6-7

The prophet Isaiah foretells the coming of the Savior.

HE PEOPLE WHO WALKED IN DARKNESS HAVE SEEN A GREAT LIGHT; THOSE WHO DWELT IN THE LAND OF THE SHADOW OF DEATH, UPON THEM A LIGHT HAS SHINED. FOR UNTO US A CHILD IS BORN, UNTO US A SON IS GIVEN; And the government will be upon His shoulder. And His name will be called Wonderful, Counselor, Mighty God, Everlasting Father, Prince of Peace. Of the increase of His government and peace There will be no end, Upon the throne of David and over His kingdom, To order it and establish it with judgment and justice From that time forward, even forever. The zeal of the Lord of hosts will perform this.

CAROL: "Unto Us a Boy Is Born"

Unto Us a Boy Is Born

1 Un - to us a boy is born! King of all cre - a - tion, Came he to a
2 Cra - dled in a stall was he With sleep - y cows and ass - es; But the ver - y
3 Her - od then with fear was filled: "A prince," he said, "in Jew - ry!" All the lit - tle
4 Now may Mar - y's son, who came So long a - go to love us, Lead us all with

world for - lorn, The Lord of ev - 'ry na - tion.
beasts could see That he all men sur - pas - es.
boys he killed At Beth - l'em in his fu - ry.
hearts a - flame Un - to the joys a - bove us.

Words: Latin, 15th cent.; tr. *Oxford Book of Carols*
Reprinted by permission of Oxford University Press.

Music: *Piae Cantiones*; arr. Geoffrey Shaw

THE FOURTH LESSON: Isaiah 11:1-9

The peace that the Christ will bring is foreshown.

HERE SHALL COME FORTH A ROD FROM THE STEM OF JESSE, AND A BRANCH SHALL GROW OUT OF HIS ROOTS. THE SPIRIT OF THE LORD SHALL REST UPON HIM, THE SPIRIT OF WIS-DOM AND UNDERSTAND-ING, THE SPIRIT OF COUN-SEL AND MIGHT, THE SPIRIT OF KNOWLEDGE AND OF THE FEAR OF THE LORD.

HIS DELIGHT IS IN THE FEAR OF THE LORD, AND HE SHALL NOT JUDGE BY THE SIGHT OF HIS EYES, NOR DECIDE BY THE HEARING OF HIS EARS; BUT WITH RIGHTEOUSNESS HE SHALL JUDGE THE POOR,

And decide with equity for the meek of the earth;
He shall strike the earth with the rod of His mouth,
And with the breath of His lips He shall slay the wicked.
Righteousness shall be the belt of His loins,
And faithfulness the belt of His waist.

The wolf also shall dwell with the lamb,
The leopard shall lie down with the young goat,
The calf and the young lion and the fatling together;
And a little child shall lead them.
The cow and the bear shall graze;
Their young ones shall lie down together;
And the lion shall eat straw like the ox.
The nursing child shall play by the cobra's hole,
And the weaned child shall put his hand in the viper's den.
They shall not hurt nor destroy in all My holy mountain,
For the earth shall be full of the knowledge of the Lord
As the waters cover the sea.

CAROL: "The Holly and the Ivy"

Individuals may sing the stanzas, with everyone joining in at the chorus.

The Holly and the Ivy

1 The hol-ly and the i - vy, When they are both full grown, Of
2 The hol-ly bears a blos - som, As white as li - ly flow'r, And
3 The hol-ly bears a ber - ry, As red as an - y blood, And
4 The hol-ly bears a prick - le, As sharp as an - y thorn, And
5 The hol-ly bears a bark, As bit - ter as the gall, And

all the trees that are in the wood, The hol - ly bears the crown:
Mar - y bore sweet Je - sus Christ, To be our dear Sav - ior:
Mar - y bore sweet Je - sus Christ, To do poor sin - ners good:
Mar - y bore sweet Je - sus Christ, On Christ - mas Day in the morn:
Mar - y bore sweet Je - sus Christ, For to re - deem us all:

The ris - ing of the sun and the run - ning of the deer, The

play - ing of the mer - ry or - gan, Sweet sing - ing in the choir.

Words and music: Traditional English

THE FIFTH LESSON: Luke 1:26-33, 38

The angel Gabriel visits the virgin Mary.

IN THE SIXTH MONTH THE ANGEL GABRIEL WAS SENT BY GOD TO A CITY OF GALILEE NAMED NAZARETH, TO A VIRGIN BETROTHED TO A MAN WHOSE NAME WAS JOSEPH, OF THE HOUSE OF DAVID. THE VIRGIN'S NAME WAS MARY. AND HAVING COME IN, THE ANGEL SAID TO HER, "REJOICE, HIGHLY favored one, the Lord is with you; blessed are you among women!" But when she saw him, she was troubled at his saying, and considered what manner of greeting this was.

Then the angel said to her, "Do not be afraid, Mary, for you have found favor with God. And behold, you will conceive in your womb and bring forth a Son, and shall call His name Jesus. He will be great, and will be called the Son of the Highest; and the Lord God will give Him the throne of His father David. And He will reign over the house of Jacob forever, and of His kingdom there will be no end."

Then Mary said, "Behold the maidservant of the Lord! Let it be to me according to your word." And the angel departed from her.

CAROL: "Ding, Dong, Merrily on High"

Ding, Dong, Merrily on High

(unison)

1 Ding dong! mer-ri-ly on high The bells are gai-ly ring-ing;
2 Ding dong! Car-ol all the bells. A-wake now, do not tar-ry!
3 Ring our mer-ry mer-ry bells, The an-gels all are sing-ing.
4 Hark now! Hap-pi-ly we sing, The an-gels wish us mer-ry!

Ding dong! hap-pi-ly re-ply The an-gels all a-sing-ing.
Sing out, sound the good no-els, Je-sus is born of Mar-y.
Ding dong! Swing the stee-ple bells, Sound joy-ous news we're bring-ing!
Ding dong! Danc-ing as we bring Good news from vir-gin Mar-y.

Glo - - - ri-a! Ho-san-na in ex-cel-sis.

Words: Traditional English

Tune: *Orchésographie*, 1588

THE SIXTH LESSON: Luke 2:1-7

The birth of Jesus takes place in Bethlehem.

AND IT CAME TO PASS IN THOSE DAYS THAT A DECREE WENT OUT FROM CAESAR AUGUSTUS THAT ALL THE WORLD SHOULD BE REGISTERED. THIS CENSUS FIRST TOOK PLACE WHILE QUIRINIUS WAS GOVERNING SYRIA.

So all went to be registered, everyone to his own city. And Joseph also went up from Galilee, out of the city of Nazareth, into Judea, to the city of David, which is called Bethlehem, because he was of the house and lineage of David, to be registered with Mary, his betrothed wife, who was with child.

So it was, that while they were there, the days were completed for her to be delivered. And she brought forth her firstborn Son, and wrapped Him in swaddling cloths, and laid Him in a manger, because there was no room for them in the inn.

CAROL: "What Child Is This"

What Child Is This

1 What child is this, who, laid to rest, On Mar-y's lap is sleep-ing?
2 Why lies he in such mean es-tate Where ox and ass are feed-ing?
3 So bring him in-cense, gold, and myrrh; Come, peas-ant, king, to own him.

Whom an-gels greet with an-thems sweet While shep-herds watch are keep-ing?
Good Chris-tian, fear; for sin-ners here The si-lent Word is plead-ing.
The King of kings sal-va-tion brings; Let lov-ing hearts en-throne him.

This, this is Christ the king, Whom shep-herds guard and an-gels sing;
Nails, spear shall pierce him through, The cross be borne for me, for you;
Raise, raise the song on high, The vir-gin sings her lul-la-by;

Haste, haste to bring him laud, The babe, the son of Mar-y!
Hail, hail the Word made flesh, The babe, the son of Mar-y!
Joy, joy, for Christ is born, The babe, the son of Mar-y!

Words: William C. Dix   Music: English ballad, 16th cent.

THE SEVENTH LESSON: Luke 2:8-16

Shepherds hear of Jesus' birth and find him lying in a manger.

NOW THERE WERE IN THE SAME COUNTRY SHEPHERDS LIVING OUT IN THE FIELDS, KEEPING WATCH OVER THEIR FLOCK BY NIGHT. AND BE-HOLD, AN ANGEL OF THE LORD STOOD BEFORE THEM, AND THE GLORY OF THE LORD SHONE AROUND THEM, AND THEY WERE GREATLY AFRAID. THEN THE angel said to them, "Do not be afraid, for behold, I bring you good tidings of great joy which will be to all people. For there is born to you this day in the city of David a Savior, who is Christ the Lord. And this will be the sign to you: You will find a Babe wrapped in swaddling cloths, lying in a manger."

And suddenly there was with the angel a multitude of the heavenly host praising God and saying:

"Glory to God in the highest,
And on earth peace, good will toward men!"

So it was, when the angels had gone away from them into heaven, that the shepherds said to one another, "Let us now go to Bethlehem and see this thing that has come to pass, which the Lord has made known to us." And they came with haste and found Mary and Joseph, and the Babe lying in a manger.

CAROL: "The First Noel"

The First Noel

1 The first No - el the an - gel did say Was to cer - tain poor shep - herds in fields as they lay;
2 They look - ed up and saw a star Shin - ing in the east be - yond them far;
3 And by the light of that same star Three wise men came from coun - try far;
4 This star drew near to the north - west, O'er Beth - le - hem it took its rest;
5 Then en - tered in those wise men three Full rev' - rent - ly on bend - ed knee,

In fields Where they lay, keep - ing their sheep, On a cold win - ter's night that was so deep.
And to the earth it gave great light, And so it con - tin - ued both day and night.
To seek for a king was their in - tent, And fol - low the star wher - ev - er it went.
And there it did both stop and stay Right o - ver the place where Je - sus lay.
And of - fered there in his pres - ence Their gold, and myrrh, and frank - in - cense.

No - el, No - el, No - el, No - el! Born is the King of Is - ra - el.

Words and music: English carol, c. 17th cent.

THE EIGHTH LESSON: Matthew 2:1-11

Wise men are led by a star to Jesus.

AFTER JESUS WAS BORN IN BETHLEHEM OF JUDEA IN THE DAYS OF HEROD THE KING, BEHOLD, WISE MEN FROM THE EAST CAME TO JERUSALEM, SAYING, "WHERE IS HE WHO HAS BEEN BORN KING OF THE JEWS? FOR WE HAVE seen His star in the East and have come to worship Him."

When Herod the king heard these things, he was troubled, and all Jerusalem with him. And when he had gathered all the chief priests and scribes of the people together, he inquired of them where the Christ was to be born.

So they said to him, "In Bethlehem of Judea, for thus it is written by the prophet:

'But you, Bethlehem, in the land of Judah,
Are not the least among the rulers of Judah;
For out of you shall come a Ruler
Who will shepherd my people Israel.' "

Then Herod, when he had secretly called the wise men, determined from them what time the star appeared. And he sent them to Bethlehem and said, "Go and search diligently for the young Child, and when you have found Him, bring back word to me, that I may come and worship Him also."

When they heard the king, they departed; and behold, the star which they had seen in the East went before them, till it came and stood over where the young Child was. When they saw the star, they rejoiced with exceedingly great joy. And when they had come into the house, they saw the young Child with Mary His mother, and fell down and worshiped Him. And when they had opened their treasures, they presented gifts to Him: gold, frankincense, and myrrh.

CAROL: "In the Bleak Midwinter"

In the Bleak Midwinter

1. In the bleak mid-win-ter, frost-y wind made moan, earth stood hard as i-ron, wa-ter like a stone; snow had fall-en snow on snow, snow on snow, in the bleak mid-win-ter, long a-go.

2. Our God, heaven can-not hold him, nor earth sus-tain; heaven and earth shall flee a-way when he comes to reign: in the bleak mid-win-ter a sta-ble-place suf-ficed the Lord God in-car-nate, Je-sus Christ.

3. An-gels and arch-an-gels may have gath-ered there, cher-u-bim and ser-a-phim throng-ed the air; but his moth-er on-ly, in her maid-en bliss, wor-shiped the be-lov-ed with a kiss.

4. What can I give him, poor as I am? If I were a shep-herd, I would bring a lamb; if I were a wise man, I would do my part; yet what I can I give him; give my heart.

Words: Christina Rossetti   Music: Gustav Theodore Holst

THE NINTH LESSON: John 1:1-14
St. John unfolds the great mystery of the Incarnation.

In the beginning was the Word, and the Word was with God, and the Word was God. He was in the beginning with God.

All things were made through Him, and without Him nothing was made that was made. In Him was life, and the life was the light of men. And the light shines in the darkness, and the darkness did not comprehend it.

There was a man sent from God, whose name was John. This man came for a witness, to bear witness of the Light, that all through him might believe. He was not that Light, but was sent to bear witness of that Light.

That was the true Light which gives light to every man who comes into the world. He was in the world, and the world was made through Him, and the world did not know Him. He came to His own, and His own did not receive Him.

But as many as received Him, to them He gave the right to become children of God, even to those who believe in His

name: who were born, not of blood, nor of the will of the flesh, nor of the will of man, but of God.

And the Word became flesh and dwelt among us, and we beheld His glory, the glory as of the only begotten of the Father, full of grace and truth.

CAROL: "Oh, Come, All Ye Faithful"

Oh, Come, All Ye Faithful

1 Oh, come, all ye faith-ful, Joy-ful and tri-um-phant! Oh, come ye, oh, come ye to Beth-le-hem; Come and be-hold him, Born the king of an-gels;

2 The high-est, most ho-ly, Light of light e-ter-nal, Born of a vir-gin, a mor-tal he comes; Son of the Fa-ther Now in flesh ap-pear-ing!

3 Sing, choirs of an-gels, Sing in ex-ul-ta-tion, Sing, all ye cit-i-zens of heav-en a-bove! Glo-ry to God in the high-est:

4 Yea, Lord, we greet thee, Born this hap-py morn-ing; Je-sus, to thee be all glo-ry giv'n! Word of the Fa-ther, Now in flesh ap-pear-ing:

Oh, come, let us a-dore him, Oh, come, let us a-dore him, Oh, come, let us a-dore him, Christ the Lord!

Words: attr. John F. Wade; tr. composite

Music: attr. John F. Wade

LEADER: The Lord be with you.

PEOPLE: And also with you.

LEADER: Let us pray. O God, who called shepherds before all others to the cradle of your Son: Grant that by the preaching of the gospel the poor, the humble, and the forgotten may know that they are at home with you; through Jesus Christ our Lord.

PEOPLE: Amen

Other prayers may be added.

LEADER: The almighty and merciful Lord, the Father, the Son, and the Holy Spirit, bless us and keep us.

PEOPLE: Amen

A History of the Service

The Service of Lessons and Carols, which many churches use during their Christmas festivities, is sometimes thought to be quite old. Actually it is of fairly recent origin. Its model is the service that comes from King's College in Cambridge, England, every Christmas Eve. That service was introduced at King's College in 1918.

The immediate origins of the King's College service reach back to 1880, to the cathedral of Truro in England's southernmost county of Cornwall. There, in a temporary wooden building, used while a new cathedral was being built, the Service of Lessons and Carols was introduced. It replaced another carol service, which two years earlier had taken the place of a custom in which the Truro choir sang carols in the community on Christmas Eve.

Though the immediate roots of the Service of Lessons and Carols are recent, the structure of the service is deeply embedded in Judeo-Christian practice and follows an ancient custom of placing music between scripture readings. One example of this custom is evident in the liturgy for Holy Communion where the Old Testament, Epistle, and Gospel readings are interspersed with the singing of a psalm and an alleluia or a verse. The roots of that practice go back to synagogue worship before the time of Jesus' birth.

A more complete and elaborate example of this practice developed from Morning and Evening Prayer, also known as matins and vespers. In these daily services readings may be followed by responsories. The Holy Week office of Tenebrae, a form of which is now used by some churches on Good Friday evening, grew from Morning Prayer. (The reason a morning service migrated to the evening is because it was said in anticipation the night before to make it easier for people to participate.) A series of nine lessons are followed by beautifully florid responsories, some of which may date from the seventh, eighth, and ninth centuries.

The Service of Lessons and Carols follows this same pattern. It grew out of a service of nine lessons for matins on Christmas Day, parallel to the Tenebrae service. As his son reported, E. W. Benson, who at the time was Bishop of Truro Cathedral in Cornwall, took the service for matins and from it "arranged . . . a little service for Christmas Eve—nine carols and nine tiny lessons. . . ."* The Rev. G. H. S. Walpole, who had originally conceived the idea, conducted the choir at the service's first occurrence in 1880 at the Cathedral of Truro's makeshift building. At the time, Walpole was Succentor (subchanter or assistant to the precentor) at Truro. He later became Bishop of Edinburgh, and Bishop Benson became Archbishop of Canterbury.

In 1918 Dean Eric Milner-White and organist Arthur H. Mann introduced this service at King's College in Cambridge. The following year Milner-White made some revisions. He prefaced the service with the Christmas Bidding Prayer and the Lord's

---

* Ray Robinson, "The Service of Lessons and Carols," *Choral Journal* 31:5 (December 1990), p. 14.

King's College Chapel, Cambridge, England (R. Richardson/H. Armstrong Roberts)

Prayer, removed the Magnificat and the benedictions between lessons, and made the prologue to John's gospel the climax of the service as the ninth lesson. The resulting form of the service has remained virtually the same since 1919, though some of the music has, of course, changed from year to year.

The King's College Service of Lessons and Carols has caught the popular imagination, especially through its airings on radio and television. Many churches have followed the service as closely as possible; some have adapted it by changing the lessons or otherwise altering it to fit their own needs and desires. One can find the service, therefore, in many different churches and in many different versions.

The service presented here is adapted for use in the home. The traditional lessons, however, have not been changed, and the King's College format and bidding prayer are still present. The carols themselves also show a healthy English influence—two of which appear where they have almost invariably been placed: "Once in Royal David's City" at the beginning and "Oh, Come, All Ye Faithful" after the ninth lesson. The final prayer, not without English influence, is one of the collects for Christmas Eve from the *Book of Common Worship* of the Church of South India.

The word *carol* can be used in a technical sense to refer to a medieval song, for any season of the year, with a refrain called a *burden*. In popular usage today *carol* has come to mean all sorts of hymns or songs, with or without refrains, which relate mostly to Christmas. Services of lessons and carols tend to use *carol* in this latter sense, as does the service presented on the preceding pages.

The carols that have been chosen are ones that can be sung at home. They do not require trained choirs or cathedral-like settings. They can be sung by everyone with the elemental and healthy vigor that all human beings long to express in song. The birth of Christ evoked and still evokes song, and everyone is invited to join in that song. So, sing with thanks and joyous abandon!

—Paul Westermeyer

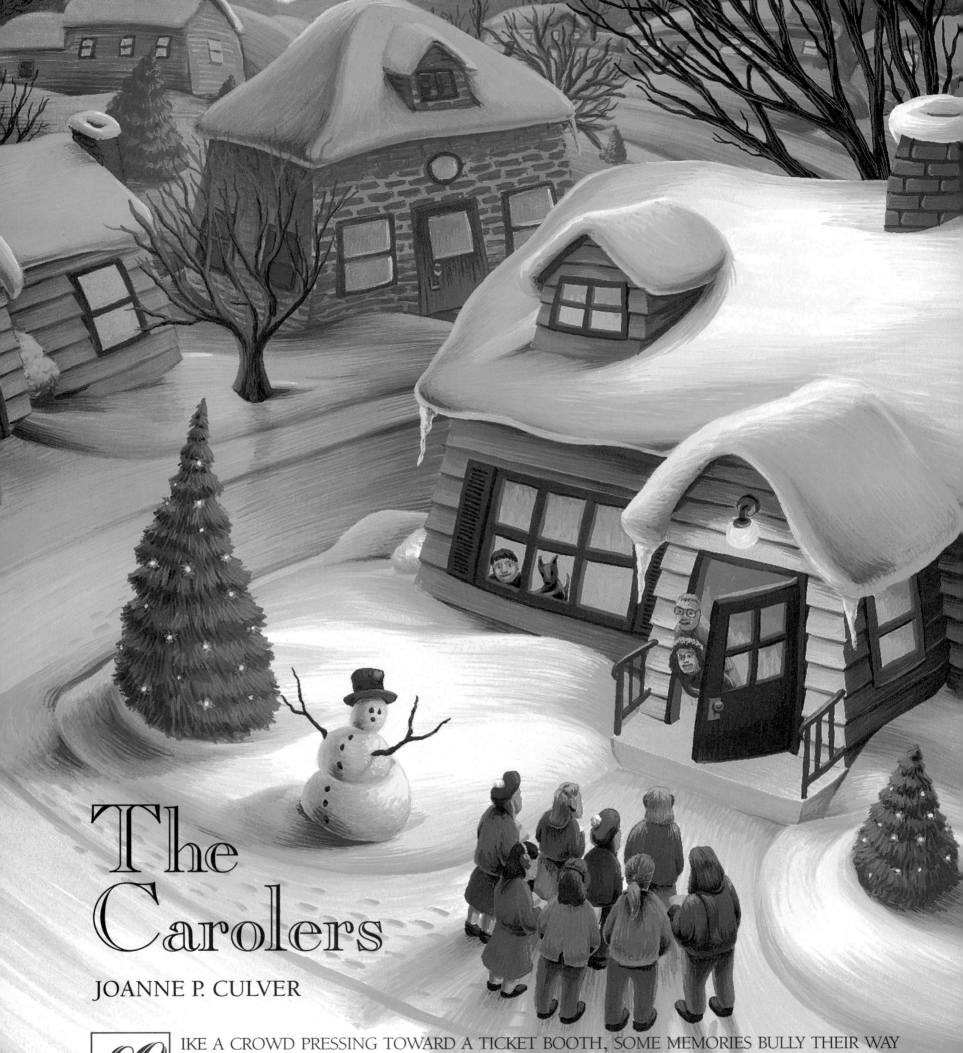

The Carolers

JOANNE P. CULVER

LIKE A CROWD PRESSING TOWARD A TICKET BOOTH, SOME MEMORIES BULLY THEIR WAY INTO YOUR CONSCIOUSNESS. OTHER MEMORIES RESIST BEING DRAWN UP AT ALL, LIKE A GIANT FISH SNARED ON A LIGHT TACKLE. WHEN YOU ARE TRULY BLESSED, SOME MEMORIES REMAIN QUIETLY WITHIN YOU, SLOWLY UNFOLDING THROUGHOUT THE YEARS UNTIL, AT GOD'S APPOINTED TIME, THEY BLOSSOM INTO FULL UNDERSTANDING. SUCH IS THE MEMORY OF CHRISTMAS 1959, MY SEVENTH-GRADE YEAR.

December 1959 in Cedar Rapids, Iowa, was cold and the color of gray. The Cedar River, which divides the city, had begun to freeze over, giving its surface the look of a black and white paint horse. Downtown, the dullness of a gray sky only enhanced the display of colored Christmas lights reflecting in long rainbow ribbons across the tops of snowbanks and down the frozen streets.

People locked their doors against December. I could not wait to participate in it. With everyone inside, December and I were left alone to discover one another. Ice skating to school after an ice storm, sledding down steep hillsides in weather thirty degrees below zero— these were the fun things of December! But the quiet things of December were dearer to me. A small hole dug into the side of a snowbank offered a warm, secret place where I could watch a squirrel track his way to a secret stash of nuts or I could curl up and take an overwhelming nap. Sharp winds wrestled with the black fingers of a barren tree. Elves carved the icicles hanging from the gutters and windows. Fairies etched their swirling dances across the frost on our windows. I felt close to God's creation in December.

As I walked down the shoveled sidewalks toward home, the color of butter oozed from my neighbors' windows as they switched on their evening lights. We lived in the second story of a white

wood-framed house. An enclosed, steep stairwell in the back was our private access to the upstairs. Bounding up the stairs, my feet and knees numb from the cold, I could smell nutmeg, the fragrance of December! Straight at the top of the stairs, a door opened into the kitchen. When I entered the kitchen, to my joy, every countertop and table was filled with cookies!

"Hey, Mom, whatcha cookin?" I asked, wrestling off my snowboots.

"Nutmeg bars," she said. "And don't get that snow all over the kitchen floor!"

"Mom, ya know what?" I asked. "Jamie says your nutmeg bars are the best in the whole world! Do you think she could take some home with her after the party?"

"Don't see why not. I

already made some extra," she replied, smiling as I snatched one off the tray.

That year Mom had allowed me to have my first caroling party. Jamie, my very, very, very best friend, and six other girls would be coming. A total of eight girls with the strongest voices this side of heaven were going to set this neighborhood on fire with Christmas spirit! I had chosen all the carols and mapped out all the homes we would visit. After caroling, we would come

back to the house for nutmeg cookies and hot chocolate.

By eight o'clock, all my friends had gathered at my house. I issued orders like an army drill sergeant and passed out little music books. We gathered at the front door, buttoning up our wool coats and pulling on snowboots.

"Remember your boundaries," Mom said with firmness. "You are not to go too far from the house, just a couple of blocks."

Completely ignoring that advice, we tumbled down the stairs and out into the night. With that first taste of cold air through my wool scarf, I sensed that this evening was special. The stars seemed to shine sharper this evening and the air hung heavy with anticipation. Snow crunched beneath our boots as we hurried down the street. We really surprised a lot of neighbors. Everywhere we went, families would gather by an open door or a big window and listen as our carols bounced off the houses up into the night sky. Some people gave us little gifts of cookies and candies. It felt good to bring happiness to others. Bubbling over with our success, we began our long walk back to the house.

"Jamie, let's take a walk past the old mansion on our way home!" I challenged.

"No way. Are you crazy?" she hollered into the night. "That place is spooky in the daytime and you want to go there at night? Besides, it's too far from your house. Remember your boundaries!"

Rats! She seemed determined not to go. Now my other friends were curious. Rachel wanted to know if anyone had gone there at night. Kim wanted to know *why* anyone would go there at night! I dared; I pleaded. Then I resort-

> ## "Let's take a walk past the old mansion on our way home!" I challenged.

ed to the lowest form of black-mail—guilt!

"Here it is Christmas!" I wailed. "You won't even go and sing for these people! I bet no one has ever sung to whoever it is in that big, old house," I pleaded, knowing full well that it was my sense of adventure that guided me and not my sense of good will.

"Oh yeah?" said Jamie. "Maybe they did go and never came out!" All of the girls readily agreed with Jamie.

"You're all just a bunch of sissies!" I hollered. I was really mad now and they knew it. "I'll go alone and you can just go on home!" I pouted and kicked the snow.

Then soft-hearted Rachel began to cry. "We don't want you to go alone. And we don't want to go home either!"

I had to hide my smile as I heard their hesitant footsteps coming up behind me. Manipulation was soooo easy! That kind of power made me even more headstrong.

The old home was set about the length of a football field back from the street. The long driveway made a huge U down one side of the front yard, across the front of the mansion, and then back down the other side to the street. As luck would have it, the black metal gates across the driveway were opened. The huge grounds were dotted with evergreens and hardwood trees. As the wind blew through their branches, they bent down and seemed to reach out toward us! Even with full moonlight on the snow, it seemed the darkest night we had ever known.

Without prompting, we all talked in whispers. We kept turning around to look behind us, feeling that we were being followed. Our shuffling feet fought every step toward the big house until there we were, staring at a huge front door. A

brass doorknocker hung on the twelve-foot door. Peering into the opaque glass of the doors, the entrance seemed to be filled with fog.

"I'm gonna be sick." wailed Jamie. "What if they kill us!"

"Oh, don't be such a baby," I whispered as my trembling hand reached for the door-knocker.

The banging of the door-knocker was completely muf-

The banging of the doorknocker was completely muffled by the pounding of my heart in my ears.

fled by the pounding of my heart in my ears. My mind was whirling! What if Jamie was right? They will probably stuff us into the walls of this place and Mom will never know we were here! Slow footsteps approached from within and we could see a dark form approach the glass of the door. We all held our breath. A turn

of the doorknob and a squeak of the hinges pierced the night and made us grit our teeth.

"Well, good evening and merry Christmas, girls!" said a soft, melodious voice. "What can I do for you?"

We stood there like zombies, staring at the sweetest face topped with curly, silver hair that reflected the soft blue color of the dress draped on her tiny body. The shock of

our imagination meeting reality left us dumb. This was no Frankenstein; this was Frank's granny!

"Uh,...we come to sing for you some carols," stammered Rachel.

I shot her my best icy stare! What English! I thought.

"If it would be all right with you," I began in my best,

most polite manner, "we would like to sing some Christmas carols."

"Well, ah, I don't know," she said hesitantly. "My brother has been ill for some time. You would have to step inside."

My imagination took off like a rocket. The spider was telling the fly to come in and sing! Clearly it was time to leave.

"What's the matter, Joanne?" purred Jamie. "Gonna chicken out, now?"

All the girls were challenging me now. Backing out would be a sure sign of cowardice. This scheme was my idea; therefore, it was up to me to follow through. I was caught in the web of my own manipulation!

Reluctantly I answered, "We can step inside to sing, but you'll have to leave the door cracked open and let us stand by it. Okay?"

To our surprise, the little lady agreed. She ushered us inside, carefully cracked the door open, and placed us in front of it.

"Just a moment, girls!" she chirped happily. "I'll go and get Brother. Just be a moment!" With that, she disappeared into the vastness of the old house.

Our noses were filled with the fragrance of musty old books and coffee. The entry in which we were standing was three stories tall with a big, winding staircase spiraling up the center of the room. A heavily carved railing trailed above the staircase. It reminded me of a long snake climbing up toward the darkness of the ceiling. The floor was highly polished marble and captured the sparkle of an overhead chandelier, which cascaded down in layers of frozen crystal.

Standing in the bright bubble of the entry, I sensed that the rest of the house was cold

and empty of people. Our whispers skipped across the hard floor and dissolved before they could reach the far walls. The rooms to the right and left were filled with the dark shadows of old furniture that Mom would say was valuable. It was all unappealing to me. Too quiet; too still.

Kim whispered our thoughts. "Don't you think we should go?" she asked, grabbing Rachel's hand for assurance.

As we pressed closer together, our faces showed a quiet anxiety. Before we could turn and exit, a faint squeaking noise floated into the room. From the darkness emerged the lady pushing her brother in a wheelchair. He seemed even smaller than us; so thin and frail. His huge brushy eyebrows arched high and framed eyes that were bright with excitement. He smiled at us. We all politely smiled back. With a nod of her head, the lady told us to begin our caroling.

We started out timidly. "Away in a manger, no crib for a bed...." They did not move, but their lips followed the words. As the spirit of the carols took hold, "God rest you merry, gentlemen, let nothing you dismay...," we grew bolder. By the time our final carol was sung, "It came upon a mid-

night clear...," we had all the confidence of a host of angels. The tall ceiling and hard marble floor created an echo chamber for our songs and magnified our eight voices into a hundred.

"Marvelous, girls!" said the lady smiling. "Please sing some more!" Then we noticed them—big, fat tears in the old man's eyes. Soon those tears became shiny streamers down his cheeks, rolling off his chin onto his housecoat. Aching knots formed in our throats. One by one, Jamie, Kim,

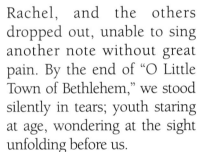

Crunching down the long driveway, I noticed some profound changes. The evergreens and hardwood trees that had tried to grab us earlier were now objects of great beauty in the moonlight. I no longer had a sense of being followed but a deep sense of being filled.

Rachel, and the others dropped out, unable to sing another note without great pain. By the end of "O Little Town of Bethlehem," we stood silently in tears; youth staring at age, wondering at the sight unfolding before us.

"Please don't stop," the man pleaded. "No one has

ever come to sing for me. What a beautiful Christmas gift, girls! Do you know my favorite, 'O Holy Night'?"

All eyes turned to me. Clearing the stiffness out of my throat, I began to sing: "O holy night, the stars are brightly shining...." Throughout the song, I determined not to look at the old man because his tears would wrench my throat. "A thrill of hope the weary world rejoices, For yonder breaks a new and glorious morn." My eyes searched the upper reaches of the stairwell, "Fall on your knees, Oh, hear the angel voices!" but eventually came to rest on the brother and sister. They were smiling! My heart lifted and my song grew bolder. "O night, O holy night, O night divine!"

Total silence. Something significant had just happened.

None of us were able to identify it; none of us knew how to receive it. Our little lady in the blue dress broke the silence.

"I think," she began, "this has been the very finest Christmas in a long time. I don't know how to thank you."

"Come here, young lady," her brother said, motioning me forward.

Slowly I walked to the side of his wheelchair. He grabbed my hand so tightly it frightened me. Then, placing my hand on his chest, he said, "In my heart I know that heaven sang with you tonight."

I stumbled back a bit and began to say how it was no big deal and our pleasure and so forth. We mumbled our goodbyes and turned toward the big front door, anxious to escape our lack of understanding. As the cold night air filled our lungs we breathed a deep, silent sigh of relief.

Crunching down the long driveway, however, I noticed some profound changes. The evergreens and hardwood trees that had tried to grab us earlier were now objects of great beauty in the moonlight. I no longer had a sense of being followed but a deep sense of being filled. Together with my friends I laughed as we made our way back to my house and Mom's nutmeg cookies.

The Boys Choir of Harlem

THOMAS GOULDE

As December's dusk settles into New York City, the lamps above Martin Luther King Blvd. flicker then wax with an electric whine as if harried awake by the fitful honking of crosstown traffic. From below, the patter of hawkers rises and falls with the call of greetings, laughter, and the din of commerce in any of a dozen languages, dialects, and accents. Here, on Harlem's great merchant thoroughfare, along sidewalks lined with vendor tables and stores festooned with lights and tinsel, streams of shoppers cross and eddy in a market scene as universal as humankind. All move to the city's beat, quickened by annual deadlines, by the shortened days, and by the chill of imminent winter, yet made buoyant by anticipation. Christmas is coming.

Walter J. Turnbull, founder and director of the Boys Choir of Harlem, is also a nationally known educator, conductor, and tenor.

Before leaving on their first European tour to Holland in 1979, the choir performs in the terminal at the J. F. Kennedy International Airport.

On their way to school , three students from the Boys Choir of Harlem Academy stop to talk on a Harlem street.

On one corner, opposite a Salvation Army bell-ringer, a Muslim tends a table of tracts and a charcoal burner in which nuggets of frankincense melt into smoke. The ancient scent drifts through the crowds, adding to the cold night air a note of remembrance and mystery. In the distance a church bell tolls.

At such an hour, in such a season, at any of a dozen churches throughout Harlem, one might hear a choir at practice. But just three blocks north, on 127th Street between Malcolm X and Adam Clayton Powell Boulevards, a very special choir may be found in rehearsal. Here, round a corner where parked cars have been known to lose their wheels, where streetlights cast into deeper pools of shadow and litter collects complacently in gutters, where in any season not all the faces are happy or friendly, the Boys Choir of Harlem makes its home in an old public school.

The holidays are an at-home time for the Touring Choir—those thirty-five or so boys who annually present upwards of ninety concerts across North America, Europe, and Asia, on trips lasting two weeks or more. This is a time for them to

be reunited with the larger fraternity of choristers, to perform locally, to be with family and friends. Returning with them is choir founder and director Walter J. Turnbull, the broad-chested Mississippian and classically trained tenor whose vision of creating an all-boy choir on the English model in the middle of Harlem, has led the choir in its twenty-four-year odyssey from a small church chorus to an internationally recognized performing arts, education, and human service organization.

This year the choir will celebrate Christmas in New York with numerous performances in various locales by several different ensembles. The boy trebles will perform in the Joffrey Ballet's production of *The Nutcracker* for a fourth sea-

son. And for a fourth year, the full, sixty-member Performing Choir will present a major Christmas concert at the World Financial Center's "Wintergarden." As usual, the Touring Choir has been booked for several corporate parties and other engagements. And continuing their tradition, both the Girls Choir and the Performing Choir will be caroling at area churches and hospitals.

Turnbull poses with four boys from the choir while on tour in Syracuse, New York.

The choir's regular concert format features three or more selections from the classical or serious modern repertoire, plus a medley of traditional Black music and a medley of popular Black music. This year, the choir has been singing Bach's cantata *Wachtet Auf* and *Ruft wuns die Stimme*, in addition to Poulenc's *Gloria*.

The traditional portion of the program is a spiritual heritage medley of four or five pieces. The medley celebrates the expressive and formal continuities of Black music from African drum chants through slave-days work songs and spirituals to modern-day gospel.

The popular section is a jazz heritage medley, comprising six to eight works that trace the ragtime and boogie-woogie roots of jazz from Scott Joplin through Fats Waller and Eubie Blake to Duke Ellington. A typical program, offering from twenty to twenty-five pieces, is packed into a solid two-hour concert (minus a fifteen-minute intermission, and plus encores).

The choir adapts the regular program throughout the year to meet the needs of specific circumstances (such as Christmas) by omitting one or more of the classical works and/or singing shortened versions of the medleys, then calling

> *What is important in the English tradition is its emphasis on the development of the individual, on awakening the best in one's character through aesthetic experience.*

upon the Performing Choir's considerable reserves to fill any gaps. Where memory can't provide, a quick study will do. These boys have, on very short notice, lofted a Hausa welcome to Nelson Mandela on his first state visit, unfurled a patriotic welcome home for Desert Storm troops, made quick lunch of a jingle for a fast-food commercial, and learned a little Russian to toast their comrades in the Leningrad Boys Choir.

It is quite a mix of music for a choir that takes as its model the English boy-choir. But choirmaster Turnbull does not hold with orthodoxy in such matters: "I

know that we are dismissed by some critics because we don't stick to the classics or to classical choral forms, but I regard the boy-choir and Western choral traditions more dynamically. What *is* important to me, and to our choristers, in the English tradition is its emphasis on the development of the individual, on awakening the best in one's character through aesthetic experience and building that self-realization through education. That, in a nutshell, is what the Boys Choir is all about. Once you understand *why* we sing, the question of what we sing assumes its proper dimensions."

In other respects, however, repertoire is of central importance. As an American choir director Turnbull encourages innovation and a degree of independence from the old forms, and works to represent American music as co-equal with European music. In his opinion, much music that is regarded as distinctly American—jazz, spirituals, gospel, blues, soul, rock and roll—would not exist without the contribution of generations of Black musicians. So naturally, the repertoire includes those sources. In the task of trying to motivate young boys, Turnbull attests that having them sing music with which they can identify proves very pro-

Members of the choir rehearse daily in order to prepare for over 100 performances a year. Choir members receive musical training as well as dance lessons.

The Boys Choir of Harlem performs a pop number. The choir's repertoire ranges from classical music to contemporary songs, gospel, and spirituals.

ductive. In his words, "No sensible choir-master would thwart such a happy development!"

The Boys Choir of Harlem has done more than simply restore neglected Black classics and folk music to the concert stage. It also has commissioned and performed new works by such Black composers as Kenny Burrell, Adolphus Hailstork, Hale Smith, and George Walker, as well as new arrangements by choir alumni M. Roger Holland, Howard Roberts, and Linda Twine.

With as least two-thirds of its program devoted to the work of Black musicians, why does the choir continue to perform the European choral classics? It's a question that gives Turnbull not a moment's pause: "Oh, there are a number of people who would have us do just that. Some of our audiences, I know, are only being politely patient during the classical segment of our concerts. They don't feel that music yet and would prefer we got on to the music with which they are more familiar. But I am a classically trained musician and am committed to awakening that sensibility in our children and, hopefully, our audiences. These are great and moving works of art, which ought to be part of everyone's experience and, I think, are a requisite of any musician's education."

Turnbull acknowledges that some critics would have his choir quit the classics, finding their voices unsuitable. These are people with an English boy-choir

sound in their ear who judge the choir according to the degree to which it can match that sound. "We don't and we won't," Turnbull says. "We are not a traditional, all-treble boys choir employing adult male tenors, baritones, and basses. We are an all-boy boys choir in which

> *In contrast to the cool, ethereal tones of a Caucasian boys choir, the Boys Choir of Harlem offers warm, resonant, lustrous voices, capable of tremendous projection even in the youngest singers.*

older boys sing those parts. And we do not teach our boys to simulate the Caucasian voice; it would be artistically illegitimate and potentially damaging to their vocal and psychological development." Instead, the boys are trained to use their voices in a natural manner so that they develop confidence in their vocal abilities and experience genuine pleasure in singing.

In contrast to the cool, ethereal tones of a Caucasian boys choir, the Boys Choir of Harlem offers warm, resonant, lustrous voices, capable of tremendous projection

even in the youngest singers. Add to this exacting standards for precision, balance, clarity, and expression, and the result is a unique and marvelous offering to the world of classical music, one that is rapidly gaining recognition.

Although he has sought it for nearly a quarter century, Turnbull is quick to assert that he is as surprised as anyone at the success and growth of the Boys Choir of Harlem. Asked to account for that success, he is liable to respond simply, "We have been fortunate."

By one reading of choir history, *need* has always impelled its development. Begun in 1968 as the Ephesus Church Choir by Turnbull (then a doctoral candidate at The Manhattan School of Music) and Ruth Nixon, the choir was to be a low-budget, after-school program for the boys of one small congregation. The need for such a program was acute and the choir was an immediate success; twenty boys enrolled the first year.

That success initiated a second motive to growth—the need to raise more money. By its second year, the choir was already concertizing in area churches and schools when Ephesus Church burned to the ground.

A third motive appeared—the need for a home. The choir moved to the Marcus Garvey Community Center in central Harlem and, as its ties to the Ephesus congregation loosened, began to change into a choir based in the broader community.

Here a fourth demand arose—the need for more comprehensive supportive services. In 1975, the choir was formally incorporated as the Boys Choir of Harlem. Four years later, while enjoying a stable residence at the Church of the Intercession in northwest Harlem, it undertook to meet the needs of young women in the community through the founding of the Girls Choir of Harlem. In 1986, the choir moved back to central Harlem into its present home in the Oberia Dempsey Multi-Service Center in order to address the educational needs of male choristers. The Boys Choir of Harlem Academy, serving 150 boys in grades four through eight, began classes in 1987.

Today, the choir is managed by twenty-three full-time staff and twenty-four part-time staff, headed by directors of operations, development, and finance.

Turnbull is still actively involved as executive director in shaping the choir's course and program, but is able to devote most of his energies to his roles as choirmaster and conductor to the Touring and Performing Choirs.

The current annual budget of two million dollars (raised from performance income, major corporate supporters, foundations, individual donors, and grants from public funds) goes to support an enrollment of 220 boys and 30 girls in its program, which encompasses the Touring Choir, the Girls Choir of Harlem, the larger Performing Choir, several boys training choirs, the academy, and a parents association. All children receive career and personal counseling (as needed), tutoring, as well as musical and vocal training. The choir has hopes of further expansion—of a girls program equal to that for boys; of an academy that will include the high school grades; of developing additional ensembles to give more children more opportunities to experience the rewards of performance.

Artistic success has been a part of the choir's history from its earliest days, but the prominence of that success has grown along with the choir's public stature. In 1979 the Boys Choir made its first European tour (Holland, France, and England), which was the subject of an Emmy Award winning documentary, *From Harlem to Haarlem: The Story of a Choirboy.* The tour was a critical success and the film sparked a great deal of public interest. The choir returned to Europe in 1982 (the second of five tours), began to tour extensively throughout North America in 1983, and in 1985 made its first tour to Asia (returning in 1989 and 1990).

Since 1986 the boy choir has taken part in four recordings plus the soundtracks of two major films, the Oscar-winning film *Glory* and Spike Lee's *Jungle Fever.* The choir also was extensively profiled in Bill Moyer's recent documentary film *Amazing Grace* and has appeared on various television programs and commercials.

It is an impressive record of accomplishment, and the Boys Choir of Harlem is committed to maintaining the momentum of its success. Such success attracts the opportunities that have allowed the choir to offset cuts in public and private funding with performance income and

also attracts interest in its core program of child development.

Once a year the Boys Choir holds auditions, which are open to all New York City schoolchildren regardless of race, although most of the more than 3000 boy

> *Of the hundreds of children who display an ability for reproducing pitch and rhythm, the choir chooses candidates who evidence the interest and commitment necessary for further development.*

and girl applicants are children of color. Of the hundreds of children who display an ability for reproducing pitch and rhythm, the choir chooses candidates who evidence the interest and commitment necessary for further development. The choir accepts dozens more than it can afford, knowing that even this select

group will be reduced by attrition.

Those that do make it are eloquent in their appreciation of what they feel the choir has done for them. Jimmy Kimbrough, who has been in the choir six of his twelve years and, like many choristers, had no sense of his own abilities before being selected, says, "I tell people that you don't have to have a gift to join; they give you the gift!" Jose Suazo, who entered the choir at the same age as Jimmy, notes the poor prospects of other kids in his neighborhood and says, "Every day I thank God, because I believe I am a blessed child for being able to be in the choir. I can't imagine my life without it." As academy students, both spend the school day at the choir but, like many of their fellows, cheerfully stay after school for tutoring, practice, and volunteer help in the choir offices.

While all feel the pressure exerted by their neighborhood peers, they have taken the measure of much that happens "on the street" and decide to let it pass. Tyree Marcus, age twelve relates, "I come home to my street and I hear, 'Oh, you finally back from that dumb choir, you so stupid to be singing and not even get paid.'" Jose answers for him, "We do get paid. We get a good education and, if we

Scholastic excellence and academic development receive the same attention as musical training at the Boys Choir of Harlem Academy. All boys in the performing choir must maintain a B average in school.

The Boys Choir of Harlem travels extensively throughout the United States and Europe each year. Choir members often travel from city to city by bus.

do well, maybe a scholarship for college." Tyree finishes his thought, "Those kids think being a big star and making a lot of money is so important, but *they* have never been on TV or out on tour."

Tracey Sydnor, who at eighteen is spending his ninth and last year with the choir, is looking forward to a career as a professional singer and composer. He feels the choir helped him understand his gifts and use his talent. "You know, even if you love to sing you can't expect to just go out and become a star. You need training. The choir has given me nine years worth of training." That training has had more than just a musical dimension, as Tracey acknowledges. "The choir does train you for real life. I think of the choir as a job. You have to show up, you have to do the work, and then you get the paycheck, which is getting to perform in public or getting chosen for a tour."

Although touring demands sacrifice and sustained concentration, it is the goal of every chorister-in-training. It may be the only means for them to visit the wider world beyond New York City and doubtless seems the way to gain the worldly poise the older boys possess.

It certainly can be broadening for young minds. Jose, who went to Japan at age nine, recalls feeling a stranger at first until the abiding friendliness of the Japanese made him feel special. He also remembers puzzling over the large, neat packages he saw on the road from the tour bus window. After some investiga-

> *The main thing about the choir and performing and Christmas is spreading peace and joy.*

tion, he determined that they contained the tools and materials of the road crews, and he was moved by the fastidious care given to such humble labor.

Tracey, who visited East Berlin at age thirteen remembers the intimidation of bus searches by heavily armed East German border guards and the awareness that he had not felt such fear before. And

he recalls the warm welcome and tearful response of his East German audience and the dawning understanding that, to them, he represented freedom.

Tyree, who feels the choir gave him the freedom to dream of possibilities and to do whatever he puts his mind to doing, had that outlook confirmed when he traveled to Hong Kong and saw "all these people living on boats!"

Jimmy, who finds every tour exciting and is still awed by the graciousness of the audiences, thinks "the audience is key to making me feel good singing, especially at Christmas when they all sing along." Jose and Tyree enthusiastically agree, as Tracey sums up, "The main thing about the choir and performing and Christmas is spreading peace and joy."

Such stories of personal insight and individual presence, when multiplied by 35, or 60, or 250, begin to give a sense of why the Boys Choir of Harlem is so special and important an institution. They also may explain why its concerts on three continents have moved both sophisticated reviewers and untutored listeners to tears of joyous affirmation.

Christmas Story Window

JEAN VANDEVENNE

The streets bustled with Christmas shoppers as Mike made his way home from kindergarten, stopping to look at nearly every shop window. He was in no hurry. His mother wouldn't be home from work for a long while.

Just around the corner of the busiest street he pressed his nose against the window of a little bookstore. The display today was not books, as one might have expected. Instead, on green burlap with sand sprinkled on it to represent streets, a little village of low, flat-roofed gray buildings nestled at the foot of a hill. Scattered about here and there were a few palm trees and some carved wood figures of people and animals.

"Oh, Mama, it's Bethlehem, isn't it!" said a little girl in a furry white hat who was standing with her mother next to Mike. "There's the inn where they didn't have any room for Jesus. Oh, and there's the stable just beyond. But it's empty. There's nobody there but some animals. How come?"

The mother thought a moment. "It looks like they just haven't arrived yet. Probably the shopkeeper will be changing things in the window every day to tell the Christmas story."

"Oh, yes, I see Mary and Joseph," the little girl said, pointing out the figures of a man and woman coming down the street with a donkey.

"And there's the shepherds and their sheep on the hillside," added a boy with a bag of newspapers slung over his shoulder who had just joined the little group. "But who's that?" He pointed to a lone figure in the very center close to the windowpane.

It was a woman, pink-cheeked and harried-looking, bent over a wooden washtub, apparently scrubbing dirty clothes with all her might. Somehow she reminded Mike of his mother.

"Who is that, Mama?" the little girl repeated the newsboy's question, tugging at her mother's coat sleeve.

"I don't know," the woman replied. "I don't remember a washerwoman in the Christmas story. Oh, there's our bus. Come on!"

The woman and the little girl got on the bus, and the newsboy ambled on down the street with his papers. Mike remained alone at the window.

So that was going to be the Christmas story, he thought. The words *Bethlehem*, *Santa Claus*, *Mary and Joseph*, *baby Jesus*, *sleigh*, and *manger* all swirled around Mike's head in a sort of Christmasy haze, but they didn't make a story. Mike decided he would keep track of the goings-on in the bookstore window and see just what the Christmas story was all about.

The next day when Mike stopped at the bookstore window the figures of Mary and Joseph stood in front of the building that the little girl with the furry hat had called the "inn." A man stood in the doorway.

The newsboy, whom Mike often saw along the street on his way home from school, had just stopped to look at the scene, too.

"You know the story?" Mike asked.

The boy looked surprised. "Sure, don't you?"

"Not all of it, I guess. What are they doing?"

"The Son of God is not going to be born in a barn, is he?"

"Well," began the newsboy, "pretty soon the lady, Mary, is going to have a baby. Only it isn't going to be just an ordinary baby; it's going to be the Son of God."

"The Son of *God*?" Mike asked in a hushed voice.

"Yes, the Son of God," the boy repeated in a matter-of-fact tone. "And now Mary and Joseph have to find a place to stay. See, they're asking at the inn—hotel, you know—and the innkeeper says, 'No, sorry, no more room.'"

"Oh," interrupted Mike, "and then the little lady washing clothes turns around and says, 'I know a good place where you can stay,' and she takes them to the nicest house in town and there the baby Son of God is born!"

"No, no," said the other boy a bit impatiently. "See that place in back of the inn? That's where he's born because there isn't room anywhere else."

"But that looks like a barn! The Son of God is not going to be born in a barn, is he?" Mike asked indignantly. "God would never let his Son be born in a place like that. I think the washerwoman will turn around and show them a nice place for the Son of God to stay."

"I don't know what *she's* doing there," the newsboy said. "But just wait, you'll see how it happened."

The next day Mike walked home briskly, sniffing now and then because the cold weather made his nose run. He didn't bother to stop at any other store windows, only giving them a glance as he went by. He was eager to see what was going on in the bookstore window.

To his surprise and disappointment, it was just as the newsboy had said. There in the stable in a little box filled with hay lay a baby. Beside him were Mary and Joseph. Gathered around, but at a respectful distance, the animals looked on.

The Son of God with no place to sleep but the cow's feed box! Mike looked reproachfully at the little washerwoman still scrubbing away over her tub. Surely she would have had a better place to give the baby to sleep. But there she was, paying no attention at all that the Son of God had to stay in a barn. Mike was relieved that the boy with the newspapers wasn't there to say 'I told you so.'

Night had come to the little village; the sky was dark blue now, sprinkled with tiny stars. Over the stable hung an especially large star. It glowed more brightly than all the others, as though somehow it had to make up for the lack of attention that the rest of the world was paying to such an extraordinary event as the birth of the Son of God. If only the little washerwoman would stop her work and turn around, Mike thought. Was she going to wash all night and never even so much as notice the bright star over the stable?

A white card with words printed on it had been added to the scene since yesterday. What did it say? Mike wondered. He studied the words. There was one he knew! Right there near the end. *John.* That was the name of a boy who sat next to him at school. And then after John were some numerals: A three with two little dots, one above the other, after it, and then a one and a six. That didn't make any sense. He hunted for another familiar word. He thought it would say *baby* somewhere—he knew that word—but it didn't. All he could read was John, three, dot, dot, one, six.

Something really exciting was going on in the bookstore window the next day after school. Angels! A lot of angels, white and gauzy, hovered in the sky above the shepherds. What were they doing? Mike wondered.

"Hey, did you see? It happened like I told you," a voice beside him interrupted his thoughts. It was the know-it-all newsboy.

Mike nodded grudgingly.

"And now the angels are telling the shepherds about the baby," the newsboy informed him. "Next, the shepherds go to Bethlehem to see the baby Jesus."

The newsboy stood there a moment, blowing on his bare hands to warm them, and then strolled on down the street.

> ## When somebody gives you a present, you pay attention and you say "thank you."

Mike pressed his nose hard against the window and looked squarely at the washerwoman.

"You'd better turn around now," he said aloud. But of course she stayed in the same spot, busy with her dirty clothes, missing the marvelous happening on the hillside not far away.

Mike thought about the shepherds. Imagine! Angels coming out of the sky—right from God probably—to tell you something. Mike felt the excitement himself. The shepherds would come as fast as they could, and all the way they would be talking about the angels and what they had said and everything.

Oh! Then it would happen! The washerwoman would hear them, and then at last she would turn around and follow them to see God's wonderful baby!

The day before Christmas, Mike hopped and skipped and ran all the way from school. With six final skips he rounded the corner and stopped short in front of the bookstore.

"Huh!" he exclaimed in breathless disappointment. It hadn't happened at all! There she was in the same old spot! That washerwoman!

He should have known. Some people were like that. Always work to do. "No, Mike," he could hear his mother say, "I can't go down and see the bookstore window tonight. I've got to get this apartment cleaned up." That was what she'd said last night.

The shepherds had left their work to go and see the baby Jesus. But angels had spoken to them. Maybe that was what it took.

Mike studied the little group in the stable. A bright, bright star and angels and a baby that was God's own Son. Wonderful happenings, this Christmas story! But why would God's baby come to that little old town and stay in a dirty old barn? It didn't make sense.

That evening Mike asked his mother, for what seemed to him the hundredth time, to come and see the Christmas story window.

"All right," she said finally. "After all, it is Christmas Eve. We ought to do something Christmasy."

Together they stood before the window, the music of carolers somewhere down the street embellishing the cold evening air.

Three new figures, colorfully dressed men on camels, had appeared at the back of the window on the left.

"The wise men," Mike's mother informed him.

He looked up at her, surprised. "You know this story?"

"Oh yes, since I was a little girl," she said. "I don't remember anything about a washerwoman, though," she added in a puzzled tone.

"Neither does anybody else," Mike said. "But those words," he pointed to the white card, "what do they say?"

"For God so loved the world," she read slowly, "that he gave his only begotten Son, that whoever believes in him should not perish but have everlasting life" (John 3:16).

"God so loved the world." Mike let the words his ears had caught run through his mind. "That little town?"

"Yes, I suppose so."

"Those shepherds?"

"Yes."

"And the washerwoman? She won't even turn around," Mike added accusingly.

"Yes," his mother said after a moment, "I guess 'the world' means everybody, even the washerwoman."

"Even you and me?"

"Why, yes," she said slowly, as though she had never thought about it before, "I guess it means you and me, too."

Just then the carolers who had been singing their way up the street, crossed the intersection and gathered themselves close to Mike and his mother. "Joy to the world," they sang, "the Lord is come! Let earth receive its King...."

Mike had never heard such music. Like the singing of angels, he thought. A warm, wonderful, glad feeling swelled up inside him and wrapped him around with joyfulness.

Then it was over. The carolers trooped on up the street. Mike and his mother again stood alone at the window. Mike felt as though all his words and all his feelings had been used up. There

seemed nothing to say and nothing to do but go home.

On the afternoon of Christmas Day Mike thumped down the stairs of the apartment building and out onto the quiet street. An aunt and uncle had come for a visit. Yet even with new Christmas toys, the day, filled with only adult talk, had grown unbearably dull. Finally, his mother had agreed that he could walk down to look at the Christmas story window.

Maybe today, Mike thought, the little washerwoman would at last stop her work and discover what was happening across the street.

But no! The wise men had gone by; there they were giving presents to the baby Son of God. And there *she* was, too busy to pay attention.

Presents for the Son of God. That was a good idea! Mike thought. But what sort of gift did one give to so special a baby?

In his mind he sorted through his own possessions, but he could think of nothing quite good enough. Not even any of his new Christmas things seemed appropriate.

Then the thought occurred to Mike that the baby himself was a present. Didn't the card say that God loved the world and *gave* his Son? The baby was God's present to the world. God's present to the washerwoman. And she wasn't even noticing!

Mike felt achingly ashamed for her. If only he could, he would reach through the glass, pick up the washerwoman, turn her around, and march her right across the street and into the barn to see God's baby.

"When somebody gives you a present, you pay attention and you say 'thank you,'" he would tell her.

But the washerwoman wasn't the only one, Mike thought suddenly. Though he didn't understand it all, he knew that here was something really important and very, very special.

God loved the world. God loved Mike. The baby was his present, too!

"When somebody gives you a present, you pay attention and you say 'thank you,'" he told himself.

Mike closed his eyes and pressed himself close to the glass. Almost it seemed as though he were part of the scene in the window, kneeling there with the shepherds and the wise men.

"I'm paying attention, God," he whispered, "and I say 'thank you.'"

A SONG IN THE DARKNESS

DOROTHY H. BIZER

Zechariah was old
and rich,
priestly and powerful,
a man of influence.

Mary was young,
and poor
innocent and unassuming,
a peasant girl.

Unwed, amazed, Mary,
with trusting heart,
leaped forth in faith
and sang with trembling joy
her song of praise,
Magnificat.

In time, acceptance and belief
to Zechariah came
and he, with Holy Spirit filled,
sang song prophetic,
Benediction.

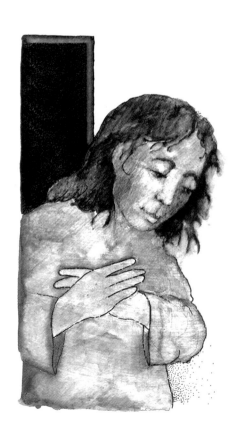

The angel Gabriel,
sent by God,
announced to both
the coming birth of sons:
"His name will be John."
"You will call his name Jesus."

With wife beyond
childbearing years,
disbelieving, Zechariah railed,
denied, and argued
until the angel
struck him dumb.

33

THE SPIDER'S GIFT

BARBARA A. MYERS

At the foot of the mountains there is a forest, a very old, very large forest that is home to many creatures. Under the trees, foxes dig their dens. Deer browse on tender green branches in the dappled shadows of summer. Rabbits at play scatter the fallen leaves; and owls hoot in the silence of moon-silvered nights.

Once upon a time, long ago, an old woman lived in the stone house that sits in the middle of the clearing. On the day before Christmas she put on her heaviest shawl, wrapped two scarves around her neck, and walked into the forest with her axe to find a Christmas tree.

A strange figure she made, all wrapped and bundled, for the snow was cold and deep in the forest. Most of the animals slept through the winter and silence lay as thick as the snow on the forest floor. The only sounds were the crunch of her boots as they broke the icy crust on the snow and the harsh warning cry of a blue jay, flying from tree to tree.

The old woman searched a long time, passing many trees. She wanted a special tree—not too tall, not too small. Christmas was a special day; not just any tree would do. At last, she found the perfect tree. The spruce was fat and fragrant and bristled with pine cones. She took out her shiny axe and began to chop it down.

At the top of the tree, hidden by the hard petals of a pine cone, a small spider had curled up for her long winter nap. The snow and the cold didn't bother her; a snug ball inside the cone, she lay fast asleep, dreaming spider dreams of summer when she would spin rainbow bridges across the forest. The little spider came from a family renowned for their spinning. Her great-great-great-grandmother had once spun a dress of shimmering, shining rainbow gauze for an elfin queen. And her great-great-great-great-grandmother was said to have spun the silken strings for an angel's harp. The little spider was sure that someday she,

too, would do something wonderful. But so far nothing had happened.

The spider was deep in her dreams when she felt the first jar as the axe bit into the tree. She lay still a moment, wondering what had woken her. Then the axe struck again, and she was almost thrown from the cone. Clinging to the needles, she crawled to the tip of the branch to look.

It was still winter, she saw with a surprise. Snow lay heaped to the lowest branches of the tree, and the wind was chill. At first she saw nothing but the snow-covered ground and the snow-frosted trees of the forest. Then she noticed a flash of silver as the old woman drew the axe back for another swing. The tree shook so hard, the spider held on with all eight legs.

The little spider didn't know about Christmas trees and axes; she just knew that something dreadful was happening. And when something dreadful is happening, the best place to be is curled up in your own bed; so she retreated to the deepest, darkest corner of her pine cone, closed her eyes, and held on tight.

Her head was spinning from all the pounding, when suddenly it stopped. The spider was about to see if the terrible woman had gone, when the tree began to sway back and forth as if rocked by storm winds. Then the whole world turned upside down, as the tree fell with a loud shuush into the deep snow.

The little spider was so stunned that she was only a bit surprised when the forest began to walk past her. She blinked and shook her head, but the great tall pines and the small, naked bushes kept right on going past. Then she realized that it was not the forest that moved. It was her own tree, crawling on its side over the snow. (She could not see the woman pulling the tree back to her house.)

The little spider was terrified. The trees were farther away now, and if she jumped off she might freeze before she could reach another shelter as warm as her pine cone. She hoped the tree knew where they were going.

In spite of the bumping and lurching, the little spider soon fell back asleep. After all, she was very tired. She usually woke at half past April.

She would have slept at least until March, but the heat and the crackling of a fire woke her. It must be spring, she thought, it is so delightfully warm. How surprised she was to find herself inside the old woman's house!

Then she saw the fire burning through a hole in the wall. The sound and smell were terrifying. But the old woman sat right beside it, rocking back and forth as she clicked a long pair of

At the top of the tree, hidden by the hard petals of a pine cone, a small spider had curled up for her long winter nap.

sticks and ignoring the danger beside her. It seemed a strange fire to the spider, for it stayed in one place and did not burn the tree or the old woman next to it. Perhaps it was like the animals that lived in people's houses and did what they were told to do.

After a while, the spider's gaze turned toward the woman and she forgot to be afraid. With the clicking sticks the woman was weaving some kind of coarse web. Why, she is a weaver, too! the little spider thought, watching the woman knit. But how slowly she weaves and what an ugly web!

Suddenly, the little spider noticed that the tree had changed. Little brown nuts and wrinkled apples had sprouted from the branches. Cautiously, she approached one of the apples. A sturdy cord held it to the branch. How strange to hang apples and nuts on a spruce tree! she thought.

Now on Christmas Eve special things can happen. When the old woman began talking to the big ginger cat rubbing against her ankles, the little spider was able to understand. "It is such a pretty little tree," the woman was saying. "How I wish I had something pretty to hang on it, instead of just walnuts and the last of my apples."

She got up and put the hat she had knitted for her friend the woodsman under the tree, along with the ball she

WHY, SHE IS A WEAVER, TOO! THE LITTLE SPIDER THOUGHT, WATCHING THE WOMAN KNIT.

had made for the cat, the packets of corn for the deer, and the bags of plump seeds for the birds.

"There, I have gifts for all my friends now. I should be so happy. I have my friends and a nice, snug house." But the more she looked at the tree, the more unhappy she became. "A Christmas tree should be special to honor the Child born this night," she told the cat with a sigh. "Wrinkled apples and old nuts just aren't special."

The cat curled in her lap and purred as the old woman rocked near the fire and surveyed the tree. A few tears slid down her wrinkled face. A Christmas tree should be special and hers wasn't. At last she fell asleep.

The little spider was sad that the old woman was so unhappy. She did not understand everything the woman had said, but she knew that this was a special night, a night of giving gifts, and that the woman was unhappy because there were no pretty things on the tree. If only there was a way to help the old woman. But what could a little spider do?

Of course! She would make the tree very special. What could be more beautiful than the fine silk of a spider web spangled with dew?

All night long, the little spider walked round and round the tree, spinning strands of silver and silk. From branch to branch, she hung her finest,

most delicate threads. Melting snow dripped through the needles and caught on the spider web, shimmering like beads in the firelight. Her great-great-great-grandmother's webs could not have been more beautiful than the one woven by the little spider on Christmas Eve.

As the tree was very tall and the spider was very small, she soon grew weary, but she did not stop. Round and round she forced her aching legs, up and down. Just a little farther, just a few more steps, she told herself, then she could sleep.

There! It was done. As she stopped to rest, her legs lost their grip and she fell to the floor. She lay on the braided rug, weeping tears of exhaustion and heaving tiny spider sobs. She didn't have the strength even to climb back onto the tree.

An angel heard the tiny sobs coming from the stone house in the snowy clearing. Folding his great wings of mingled moonlight and starlight, he entered the house. There he saw the old woman, sleeping in the chair by the dying fire, her shawl slipping from her shoulders. He saw the tree, decorated to honor the Child with its withered apples and hard, brown nuts and moon-spangled web. And he looked into the heart of the old woman and smiled.

With a touch of his hand the tree was transformed. The wrinkled apples fattened into crisp, red globes. The plain,

THE MOON SHONE ON THE TINY DROP OF A SPIDER'S TEAR AS IT BALANCED ON THE ANGEL'S FINGERTIP.

brown nuts became gilded. The pine cones glittered with snow dust that would not melt. And the spider web, oh, the spider web changed into golden scallops of garland and silvery falls of tinsel.

The little spider woke to a sight more beautiful than her brightest dreams. In fear and awe, she began to creep away into the shadows, but the angel saw her tiny movement. Bending low, his great luminous wings sweeping the hearthstones, and with infinite care he picked up the little spider and put her back in her pine cone. No longer afraid, the spider closed her eyes to spin golden dreams of gossamer and spring.

The moon peeked through the window as the angel straightened the shawl around the shoulders of the old woman. At his touch her cares lightened, and she smiled in her dreams. Then the angel bent again as he spied a bright glimmer beneath the tree. The moon shone on the tiny drop of a spider's tear as it balanced on the angel's fingertip. Like polished water, the single tear reflected the silver and gold tree, the scarlet fire, and the blue of the angel's eyes, deep as the sea and bright as the heavens.

The angel carried the tiny jewel to the throne of heaven, a gift for the Child who counts the sparrows that fall and heeds the tears of spiders and old women.

S T R A W

DAWN FINLAY

A farmer sowed some wheat one day,
in his little stoney field,
and watched it grow till harvest,
to see what it would yield.

Then when the wheat was ready and threshed,
he carried the straw away,
to sell to the man who kept the inn
where the travelers came to stay.

And never was straw so golden
or never had smelled so sweet,
as he heaped it into the manger
where the cattle came to eat.

But it had a higher purpose
than ever had straw before,
for on it would sleep the Son of God,
whom heaven and earth adore!

The Adoration

A tapestry by Morris & Company

ARTICLE BY PHILLIP GUGEL

eginning with the redesign of his own home's interior decoration, William Morris (1834-96) eventually became the most influential leader of the Arts and Crafts Movement in England. Through his firm's artistic production and his own writing, speaking, and advising, Morris tirelessly championed the necessity of affordable and beautiful art for all people, rather than for only a wealthy minority. One maxim in his philosophy of art was "Have nothing in your houses which you do not know to be useful or believe to be beautiful."

Morris's mission grew out of his reaction to the ill-designed and slickly manufactured decorative art and furniture available for sale at that time. This commercialization was due, in part at least, to the Industrial Revolution. Morris roundly criticized what he considered this decline. English craftspeople, he thought, had lost their skills and self-respect, while the art industry had grown

Photo: William Morris in a smock and hat.
(The William Morris Gallery, Walthamstow, London.)

The Adoration of the Magi. Used by permission of Norfolk Museums Service (Norwich Castle Museum).

rich manufacturing technically advanced works that were artistically lifeless.

Two key experiences sparked Morris's crusade. In 1857, the rooms he took for lodging in London were in need of repair and furnishing. Because he so disliked the furniture sold in shops, Morris sketched his own designs and had a carpenter build what he wanted. Then in 1859, Morris had his first major opportunity to use his talent for interior design when, together with Philip Webb,

a new architect and future partner in his firm, he built the famous Red House near London for his wife, Jane Burden, and himself.

As a result of these experiences, Morris and six others (among them the Pre-Raphaelite painters Ford Madox Brown and Daniel Gabriel Rossetti) founded Morris and Company in 1861. The firm's purpose was to offer the public an alternative to the bad decorative art and furnishings then sold. They sought

to provide tastefully designed and honestly crafted architectural carving, fabrics, furniture, metal work, mural decoration, and stained glass.

Tapestry weaving was among the fabric crafts Morris played a key role in reviving. Before its decline, tapestry had enjoyed great popularity in medieval and renaissance Europe. Morris liked the tactile and textural qualities of tapestry and defined it as "a mosaic of pieces of color made up of dyed threads."

tapestries that hung in the cathedrals at Amiens, Beauvais, Chartres, and Rouen, as well as in the Cluny Museum. Edward Burne-Jones, his college chum who taught him drawing and engraving, accompanied "Tops" or "Topsy" (as he called Morris) on a second tapestry viewing trip. Burne-Jones, too, had aspirations for the priesthood. So it became doubly momentous the last night of that summer vacation in France when they both decided to abandon their plans for a priestly vocation and to "begin a life of art" instead.

Henry Dearle, who became one of his gifted pupils and designers, was the first apprentice weaver Morris hired at the firm's studio on Queen's Square. Full-scale tapestry weaving did not begin, however, until the firm moved from its London location to the nearby village of Merton Abbey, the spacious quarters of a former Huguenot silk works next to a river. There three looms were set up in June 1881.

From 1878 to 1892, Morris directed the revival of the very old craft of high warp tapestry weaving, in which the warp threads are placed vertically on an upright loom. In this technique, the weaver works from the back of the tapestry, guided by looking through the warp threads at a mirror hanging in front of its design, a method used to make medieval Flemish tapestries. All designs were woven sideways, from one side to the other. During Morris's lifetime the medieval "slit" method was used, which left space at the juncture of different colors. The spaces were filled in by hand later.

Even though Burne-Jones's historical and stylistic preferences for tapestry differed from his own, Morris made him his chief designer of tapestry figures. Burne-Jones's designs, done in collaboration with Morris and Dearle, made the firm's tapestries the most artistic ones woven during the nineteenth century in England. *The Adoration* featured here is from the firm's best creative era.

Producing a tapestry like *The Adoration* required a lengthy design and weaving process. Burne-Jones began the process by making individual drawings from carefully prepared studies. The drawings of any figures in the design were never more than fifteen inches high.

From Burne-Jones's initial designs, Morris made color drawings, a task Dearle assumed in 1887. Burne-Jones then reviewed the drawings before they were sent to a London photographer, who enlarged them to their planned full size and mounted them on stretchers. Morris and Dearle next drew in the foreground and background details and made a tracing of its floral decoration and ornamentation. The complete colored drawing was called the *cartoon*. From this, the tapestry's weaver made a complete tracing of the cartoon to use on the loom.

Completion of a piece the size of 'The Adoration' was an expensive, painstaking, and time-consuming task, one not readily appreciated now.

The loom was prepared by stringing it with *warp* (the cotton string a tapestry's threads or *weft* were woven into). Then the cartoon's design was retraced on the warp in ink using a small piece of ivory with a sharp edge. These preparations could take at least two days to complete.

Tapestries were woven using a *plain-weaving* technique (picking up alternate warp threads with each weft thread). Wool, silk, and mohair fibers were used for softer highlights. The woven weft threads were tightly pushed down with a comb so that no warp threads were seen. Natural dyes gave the fibers their subdued tones, which Morris preferred. Due to his exacting technical standards, quality materials, and involved weaving process, completion of a piece the size of *The Adoration* was an expensive, painstaking, and time-consuming task, one not readily appreciated now.

Morris apprenticed boys at about age thirteen as weavers, because in his opinion, the "work of weaving is a kind which experience proves to be best done by boys. It involves little muscular effort and is best carried on by small flexible fingers." These apprentices received

Born of Welsh ancestry, Morris was fond of art, nature, and poetry. His wealthy parents intended him for the Anglican priesthood, and he read theology at Exeter College, Oxford. He was awarded only a "Pass" degree in 1856. Perhaps his low marks were due to his increasing appetite for medieval art and literature, which became his first intellectual passion.

During a visit to France on a school holiday, he studied the medieval board, lodging, and a weekly payment based on how much weaving they had completed. Their training gave them experience in and knowledge of the entire weaving process. Apprentices were required to complete a number of trial weavings to demonstrate their skill before they were allowed to work on a commissioned design. Weaving was tiring, due in part to the low bench on which a weaver sat.

If the work was demanding, so was the dress code: black-striped trousers, starched collars, vests, and black coats. This "office dress" was worn even in summer. While at the loom an overall or smock was worn; but if clients, photographers, or visitors came, the smock was removed. In today's jean, sneaker, and tee-shirt culture, employees would need bribing to wear such attire, if they would wear it at all!

The subject of *The Adoration* is the visit of the Magi, or wise men, to the Christ child and his parents. The tapestry's stately figures are arranged in two processions, which meet at the center in front of the levitating angel. Yet despite our close-up view of them, as if in a movie, the figures make no eye contact with us. They seem to inhabit an imaginary, distant land, one redolent with botanical delights.

Their enlarged features, height, and otherworldly presence is accented by the vertical folds of their clothing. Especially decorative and elaborate in contrast to the rest are the angel's priestly vesture and the second wise man's knightly apparel. All of the Magi have removed their crowns as a sign of reverence for the Christ child; that of the oldest rests on the ground before him, while his companions cradle theirs with their left hand.

Traditional elements associated with the Magi are evident. The Magi are shown as kings (denoted by their crowns), recalling the reference in Psalm 72 to kings bringing presents and adoring the Messiah. They present Jesus with containers of gold, frankincense, and myrrh. The faces—one elderly, one middle-aged, and one youthful—signify the whole range of human age united in doing homage to the Savior. The Magus

on the right continues the legend that one of the three was dark-skinned.

A thatched canopy shelters the holy infant. His parents are shown in their usual way: Joseph as a grandfatherly figure and Mary as a young woman. Influenced by the Pre-Raphaelite painters with whom both he and Morris were

Through his reliance on honest craftsmanship, Morris restored the self-respect and status of printers, weavers, and other craftspeople.

associated, Burne-Jones's figures in *The Adoration* are idealized and sentimentalized, a treatment that is generally characteristic of persons portrayed in Pre-Raphaelite religious works.

Henry Dearle's lush array of English garden flowers forms a botanical barrier between them and the mysterious woods, while his visually appealing floral and foliate border frames and sets off the tapestry's scene.

Measuring about 104 by 156 inches, this version of *The Adoration* was woven in 1906. It now hangs in the principal tower of Norwich Castle. There were at least ten versions of *The Adoration* woven between 1890 and 1907, each with a different border. The first was done for Exeter College's chapel, Burne-Jones's and Morris's alma mater. Other versions were sent as far away as Australia.

As a reformer of the decorative arts, Morris took the time to learn, revive, and modify long-forgotten methods for producing quality art. Working alongside his studio employees, he revitalized medieval ideals of the designer-craftsman. Because of his extremely high standards for the design and production of decorative arts, notable improvements in their quality and manufacture were made. Unfortunately, this prevented

Morris from selling the firm's work at prices low enough to reach a broader public; the cost of production meant that only those at a certain income level could afford them. It saddened Morris that he could not resolve the dilemma of affordable art versus high production costs in the favor of more people.

In crusading for the social and spiritual power of the visual arts, Morris made public impact. Through his reliance on honest craftsmanship at the Merton Abbey Works, "a colossal kindergarten for adults," and at the Kelmscott Press, which printed fifty-two books with his designs between 1891 and 1898, Morris restored the self-respect and status of printers, weavers, and other craftspeople. Through his leadership, the Arts and Crafts Society began in 1888 to exhibit examples of decorative art. Morris also established the Society for the Protection of Ancient Buildings in response to the alteration and destruction of historic buildings. Believing beauty to be marketable, Morris and Company purposely combined the roles of architect, interior designer, and retailer in its functions. The firm continued to operate until forced to close in early 1940 because of the war.

The remarkable spirit William Morris exerted in renewing English decorative art during the nineteenth century seems overwhelming, even though we have limited our attention here to his tapestry production. Combining a bold artistic vision, a crusading and enterprising commitment to that vision, a curious intellect with wide-ranging interests and respect for visual traditions, a compassion for craftspeople and their work, and a genius for design exercised with seemingly endless energy and enthusiasm, Morris imparted new life and quality to the decorative arts and enlarged their definition. In doing so, he fulfilled the vow he made with youthful idealism some forty years before, to pursue an artistic, rather than churchly, vocation. The energy he spent in this pursuit may have contributed to his early death at the age of sixty-two. We remain appreciative inheritors of the immensely rich and vital legacy of decorative art his devotion and sacrifice generated.

THE SWEET SMELL OF CHRISTMAS

WILDA McALISTER

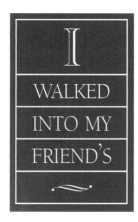

I WALKED INTO MY FRIEND'S old-fashioned kitchen the other day and could hardly see through the steam. But my nose recognized the sweet smell of plum pudding. It took me back to my childhood in England when we youngsters would gather round the stone sink to watch Mum assemble the ingredients. Our eyes fairly danced in our heads when we were allowed to share in this noble task. With scrubbed hands—similar to a surgeon's preparations—we mixed raisins, currants, citron, suet, flour, sugar, and spices. Mum herself added the liquid spirits.

Then came the stirring. Everyone must take a turn or miss out on the good luck it allegedly brought. The big event was the inserting of trinkets into the sticky concoction. With much jostling and merriment, we speculated on what unlucky female would bite into the silver thimble in her slice of pudding and thereby end up an old maid. At the other extreme, the receiver of the gold ring could begin planning her wedding.

In case enough good luck had not been stirred up, shiny coins we called "throppenny bits" were added for insurance. At length, the entire mass was swathed in heavy cloth, lowered into a kettle of boiling water, and cooked for hours. Ah, the delicious odor that permeated the house!

Plum pudding, of course, was a staple of Victorian times, but it has an earlier origin. Curiously, plums are not included in any recipe. The use of the word *plum* joined with *pudding* is obscure. It may refer to the dried plums or prunes used before the introduction of raisins. Raisins replaced prunes sometime during the Victorian era. Ground suet, though, was an ingredient in the Victorian plum pudding and is today. But the proportion of meat has decreased considerably.

A freshly killed stag may have begun plum pudding. The story goes that an English king went hunting, when he and his cook became lost in a blizzard. As the next day was Christmas, the cook determined to prepare the meal by tossing everything he had into the pot. To the remains of the stag (meat chopped fine), he added flour, apples, dried plums, eggs, ale, brandy, and sugar. After stirring, he tied the sticky mass into a bag and boiled it until it was pudding!

Beginning the pudding several weeks in advance of Christmas came about for another reason. In the *Book of Common Prayer* of the Church of England, the prayer for the last Sunday before Advent began with the words "Stir up." This the good people of Peterborough, England, took to be a reminder that they should start their plum pudding on the last Sunday before Advent. ❧

Christmas Plum Pudding

1 c. ground suet
1 c. raisins
2 c. dried bread crumbs
½ c. chopped nuts
1 c. sugar
½ c. milk

1 beaten egg
½ t. soda
1 t. cinnamon
½ t. cloves
½ t. allspice
½ t. salt

Mix all ingredients well & pour batter into a greased pudding mold. Cover. Steam 2 hours in boiling water. Be sure water is kept boiling. Unmold & serve hot with a sprig of holly in the center.

Merry Christmas, Grandfather

JACK RONALD

~

SHE HAD ALWAYS THOUGHT OF HIM AS SANTA CLAUS. BUT NOW SHE DIDN'T KNOW WHAT TO THINK.

The cream and gold 1957 Plymouth rolled through the night on U.S. 20. Rebecca sat in the darkness of the back seat, her thoughts blurred and distorted like the bright lights flashing by as the car sped past motels and gas stations and decorated storefronts. Christmas itself seemed distorted for the second year in a row.

The last Christmas Rebecca could remember enjoying, really enjoying, was the year before last. But that was before her father was transferred to his new job. It was before the move away from New York to Ohio. It was before Jeffrey, Rebecca's brother who now slept in his mother's arms in the front seat, was even born. And it was before Grandfather had changed.

Actually, thought Rebecca as she listened to the intermingling of a Chipmunk's song on the radio and her mother cooing to Jeffrey, not all of the changes had been bad ones. Her new school was more fun than her old one. Fifth grade was more fun than fourth. And even though her friends had warned her little brothers are a pain, she liked Jeffrey and enjoyed helping her parents care for him. She also liked the fact that her dad had more time to spend with her now. His new job was good if only for that reason.

What she didn't like was being away from the farm. She missed the short walk through the grove and over the stone wall to her grandparents' house. Her grandmother would be in the kitchen, with all those smells. The farmhouse was always toasty in the wintertime, especially the kitchen, and always cool in the summer, especially the cellar where her grandmother stored jars of preserves and where her grandfather had once told her stories about cutting pond ice in his boyhood.

Grandfather.

"How many more miles is it?" asked Rebecca.

Her father sighed. He wished for a moment he had kept track of how many times that question had been answered since they left home.

"Not too far now," said her mother softly, so as not to awaken Jeffrey. "Not too far. It'll be good to get back to the farm for Christmas, won't it?"

Rebecca wasn't sure. She said nothing.

"Your father's looking forward to it, anyway," said her mother. "Imagine, a grown man. I hope, Rebecca, you're lucky enough to fall in love with a man who doesn't always have to go home to his parents' for Christmas."

"Now, c'mon," said Rebecca's father, reacting with a smile to the teasing. "I don't *have* to go home for the holidays. I just *want* to. That's all. And besides, it wouldn't be Christmas if we weren't at the farm, would it?

"The farm's the place for Christmas," continued her father, his shoulders rising somewhat as if he were no longer weary from the long drive. "That old house. Did I ever tell you that when I was a kid it snowed so much one January that we were able to sled out of the second-story window of my room right onto one of the drifts?"

Rebecca's mother looked back at her and winked.

"But at Christmas," her father said, "at Christmas, it's special. There's no place like that house on our hill with family around."

"Is that why we go back every year?" asked Rebecca from the back seat.

"Because of family? Sure. These days," he said, looking for a moment at his wife, "it's especially important."

Rebecca was silent for a moment. Then, surprising herself, she said, "Because of Grandfather."

Her parents were silent. "Yes," said her father at last, "because of your grandfather. Because of my father."

Rebecca closed her eyes. She did her best to concentrate on the best Christmases ever. She remembered her grandmother and grandfather dancing in the kitchen to music on the phonograph. She remembered sleeping for the first time in the bed her father had slept in as a child.

She remembered the smell of turkey. She remembered the plum pudding, her father lighting the brandy and pouring the blue liquid fire over the moist cake, and the feel of a real English sixpence, planted in the pudding by her grandmother, when she found the good-luck piece in her first bite.

And she remembered her grandfather's laugh.

All of that was before last Christmas, she thought. Last Christmas was different.

"He's had a stroke," her mother had told her. But Rebecca didn't know what that meant. What she knew was that, last Christmas, Grandfather was somebody else.

He sat in his favorite chair, as he always did every Christmas. But last year he had to be helped into it. And there was a strange, sad stain on the upholstery behind his head, where the oil from his hair had damaged the fabric because his neck was too weak to keep him upright.

Most of the time he sat in bed. But he wasn't in his bedroom. He was in the funny room on the north side of the house that Grandmother called the "borning room."

"It's called that because," her grandmother said once, "that's where the babies are born."

But last year it didn't seem like a place for babies, and Rebecca didn't think Jeffrey had been taken in there at all.

Instead, it was like a hospital room. Grandfather's bed was, in fact, a hospital bed. His wheelchair was parked in one corner. The room did not smell like turkey or plum pudding or anything like Christmas.

Rebecca knew a lot about that room, not because she had spent a lot of time there last Christmas. In fact, she had avoided it.

But when she was there, she concentrated on the furnishings. She could tell you, for example, which crank to turn to make the bed go up or down or fold at funny angles. But she couldn't tell you for sure what Grandfather looked like last Christmas.

She had always thought of him as Santa Claus. He had had a white beard all of her life, although it wasn't as full as the ones on the Santas in the department stores. And his cheeks were perpetually rosy. And he always seemed about to laugh out loud. It was his eyes, though, that seemed most right.

But all of that was before he changed.

Last Christmas he had been a ghost Rebecca was afraid to look at. She had no idea now what he really looked like. She knew he was thinner, because she had heard her parents worrying about it. She knew he was silent now, except for strange noises she heard once or twice. And she knew. . .no, that's not the right word. . .she was afraid that she was afraid of him. She wondered what that meant about both of them.

"We're getting close," said her mother. "Here's the last turn."

The Plymouth turned right off the main highway up a narrow road and through a thicket of trees. Rebecca could see her father's shoulders rise again, as if he were growing taller.

"Our hill," he whispered. The Plymouth climbed it slowly, dipped as it made its way around a curve, then turned right into the opening between two white fence posts.

All of the lights in the farmhouse were on. Their glow spilled out onto the snow like butter. Rebecca's father turned off the engine, and a lovely silence enveloped the family.

Rebecca's mother looked back over her shoulder and spoke softly. "This may not be easy for you, I know. But it is Christmas. And it is important."

Rebecca nodded, not knowing entirely what her mother was talking about. Before she had a chance to think about it, the kitchen door flew open.

"Welcome home!" cried her grandmother. "Merry Christmas to all of you!"

Her father gave her grandmother a long hug. "How's the woman with the tiniest waist in half the state?"

"That was a long time ago," said Rebecca's grandmother. "Before you were born."

"Dad always bragged about you," said Rebecca's father, continuing the hug. He let her go. "How is he?"

"Much the same," said Rebecca's grandmother. "Come, come. It's freezing out here. Let's get all this inside. I don't want my only grandchildren to turn to ice. What would I do with all those Christmas presents?"

Rebecca grabbed her bag of books in one hand and her grandmother in the other and jumped up the stone steps into the welcoming farmhouse.

It was as toasty as ever. A fire—it looked like the same fire every Christmas in Rebecca's life—blazed in the fireplace. Garlands of evergreen were strung up the staircase. And in the parlor, out of the corner of one eye, Rebecca could see the tree.

And beyond it, she could see the yellow light of the "borning room," where she knew Grandfather was lying.

"My, how you've grown," said Grandmother. "I thought that baby would beat you, but

I swear you've grown more than he has." She held Rebecca's hands and stepped back from her. "And so beautiful. Grandfather will be so proud."

Rebecca felt herself move. Then she felt her grandmother squeeze her hands. "He will be so proud," she said softly.

Firmly, with a hand on Rebecca's spine, she steered the child through the dining room toward the yellow light.

"Look who's here, Martin! It's David and his family," said Rebecca's grandmother with too much cheer.

Rebecca felt herself being propelled into the "borning room." Planters lined one wall, some of them sporting "Get well soon" cards that had long

ago yellowed. The hospital bed occupied most of the facing wall, and most of the bed was unoccupied. That part that was occupied was taken up by Rebecca's grandfather.

She knew that because she had focused on the sheet and had seen his outline. But she still managed to avoid looking directly at him.

Her grandmother chattered on like a ventriloquist's dummy. Rebecca looked at the sides of the bed. She looked at the outline of what was, apparently, her grandfather's knee. She looked, one more time, at the planters on the far wall.

When, thought Rebecca, when will it be enough?

Finally, with the same firm hand that had guided her to the room, her grandmother gave Rebecca a pat on the head.

She was dismissed. She could go.

But for some reason, she didn't want to. She thought for a moment about looking at her grandfather or, even more, saying something to him.

In the end, she didn't. Her grandmother left the room in search of Rebecca's parents, and Rebecca escaped, unaware of whether her grandfather was awake or not.

She worked hard the rest of the night to be invisible. And it pretty much worked.

Rebecca slept that night in her father's old room, the one he claimed he had sledded from after a January blizzard long ago. Her parents, for the first time, slept in her grandparents' bedroom, with Jeffrey in a crib near their feet. She did not know where her grandmother slept.

But when she awoke, her

Rebecca wondered if anyone had noticed that to get to the parlor she went through the kitchen and the front hall rather than get too close to a certain room.

grandmother was at the foot of Rebecca's bed. "Let's go," she whispered. A conspiratorial smile crossed her face. "Let's go."

Rebecca grinned back but didn't say a word.

They hurried down the narrow stairs, dodging the creakiest steps, to the kitchen. At first they said nothing, communicating simply with hand signals, pointing at the eggs or the skillet. Then they whispered. Then, as the smells of coffee and pancakes and bacon moved like a spirit through the house, they began laughing. Their voices rose. Rebecca couldn't remember the last time her grandmother had acted so silly.

"Erg," said the man in the brown bathrobe who stood in the kitchen door. "What time is it?"

"Time to be up and about, young man," said Rebecca's grandmother.

"It's Christmas Eve, Daddy," said Rebecca.

Her father yawned and scratched his head.

"Coffee," said Grandmother. Rebecca's father took the mug, smiled at it as if remembering a story, and took a sip.

"Jeffrey slept through the night," he said. "I was afraid he'd be confused by the trip."

Grandmother pushed him toward the table. But he shook his head. "In a minute," he said, "I want to say good morning to Dad."

Rebecca stirred harder at whatever it was she was stirring. She felt her grandmother beside her after her father had left.

"Your grandfather likes a 'good morning,' I think, though it's hard to tell. It would be so much easier if he could tell us when he's happy or when he's sad or when he's bored or uncomfortable. Mostly, though, I think he's angry."

Rebecca stirred harder still but asked, "Angry?"

"*Frustrated* may be a better word," said her grandmother. "But angry too. He's mad at his body for letting him down. It's as if he wants to complain, but he doesn't know who to complain to."

Rebecca might have asked another question, but her mother appeared with Jeffrey in her arms. "Rebecca, you know the routine. I'd like you to show Grammy what we're feeding Jeffrey for breakfast these days," said her mother. "Is that Dad's?" she asked, pointing at a tray that had been prepared.

Rebecca's grandmother nodded.

"May I?" asked Rebecca's mother.

Her grandfather nodded.

The morning flew by with too much food, too many dishes, more silly jokes from her grandmother, and Jeffrey being difficult about his breakfast. In the few moments when she found herself with time on her hands, Rebecca chose her route through the house carefully. She went no closer than five paces from the door to the "borning room."

By lunchtime, the clock was slowing down. The house was getting smaller. And Rebecca wondered if anyone had noticed that to get to the parlor she went through the kitchen and the front hall rather than get too close to a certain room.

"I want to go out for a walk," she announced as the lunch dishes were being cleared.

Her mother frowned, peeking through the fogged window at the thermometer hung outside. But her father nodded okay.

It was colder than she remembered it being on Christmas Eve before. The snow squeaked and crunched. Wind blew banners and flags of snow off the roof and out of the eaves. And it was quiet. Far

quieter than their new home in Ohio.

Rebecca moved away from the farmhouse to the south; the hill sloped away toward a grove of ancient trees. Midway through the grove was a stone wall. It came to Rebecca's waist now, but she could remember when it had seemed much higher.

There were no human tracks in the snow, although it was clear that the deer and rabbits were plentiful this season. Rebecca rested against the wall.

Behind her were her own tracks and the farmhouse, ahead of her the snow in the grove was undisturbed. If she moved a little to the right, she could make out the outline of part of the roof. And she could see smoke was coming from the chimney of her old house.

Someone is having Christmas Eve there, she thought. And someone is going to have Christmas there too. It's just not fair.

She banged her fist onto the stone wall, making snow fly in all directions. She banged it again and felt her cheeks turning hot.

"It's a strong wall," said her father's voice behind her. "Your great-great-grandfather built it. And every generation has helped keep it strong. Your grandfather practically rebuilt it one year. And I've put my share of stones in place."

"It's not fair," said Rebecca aloud. Her cheeks were hotter and her eyes hurt. "I wish things were more like they were before."

Her father moved up beside her and rested his hands on the wall. The two of them watched the smoke rise from the distant chimney on the house that had once been their home.

"I like this grove," he said at last. "And I liked that house."

He smoothed his hands on the top of the wall, clearing away the snow. "I liked coming through here to see my parents, and I liked having you come through here to see your grandparents," he said. "But even though that doesn't happen anymore, I still like this grove."

Rebecca was silent.

"I followed your tracks," said her father. "You followed the path. You couldn't see it under the snow, but you followed it."

Rebecca looked at him. "It's still there, isn't it?"

Her father shrugged. He pointed to the unblemished snow on the other side of the wall. "It's over there, isn't it?" he asked. "It's covered with snow. And maybe it's covered with weeds. And maybe nobody's come this way since we moved to Ohio. But it's still over there, isn't it?"

"Sure it is," said Rebecca. "That didn't change."

"No," said her father, "that didn't change. Just because it's under the snow and nobody comes this way anymore doesn't mean it's gone. It just means we're the only ones who know how special this place is."

Rebecca stared at the grove on the other side of the stone wall for a very long time. In her mind she traced the path she had walked so many visits to the farmhouse on the hill.

"It's getting colder," said her father. "I don't want you to be sick on Christmas Day. Let's get some cocoa."

They walked back to the farmhouse in silence.

They stamped their boots on the back porch. The door slammed when they entered.

"Shhhhh! Jeffrey's napping," said Rebecca's mother.

"And so's Dad," said her grandmother.

The three adults huddled in the kitchen, muttering to one another over warm cups of coffee, sometimes laughing softly, sometimes sighing.

> *When Rebecca peeked around the corner, she saw the crumpled shape sitting up in bed. She thought again of him as a picture, as a shape, as someone she had never known.*

Rebecca sipped at her cocoa and dreamed of the days when she could walk into the kitchen and make all the noise she wanted. She imagined herself now, walking through the grove, climbing over the wall, trudging up the slope, and coming into the warm kitchen to have Christmas Eve cocoa. Her grandmother would be singing, and the laughter of her grandfather would echo through the house.

Grandfather.

She put down her cocoa and drifted out of the kitchen.

In spite of herself, she knew where she was going. In spite of herself, she found she was heading for the "borning room."

He was asleep. At least he wasn't moving. She looked at him, but at the same time she didn't really look at him. She didn't see him as Grandfather. She wasn't even sure she saw him as a person. Instead, she saw him as something to see, like a picture, or an audience when you're on stage and afraid you'll forget your lines.

He looked a little like her grandfather. The beard was still there, although it was trimmed badly. The face was drawn and hollow-looking. His cheeks were more pale than rosy. And his hands, once the strongest hands Rebecca had ever seen, were thin and skeletal and spotted with brown.

She looked at him like a picture of someone she did not know. She didn't fear him. She wasn't put off by him. It's just that he was a picture of someone she did not know.

"He doesn't look like himself, does he?" It was her grandmother. Rebecca felt herself blushing.

"It's all right, child, I know it's upsetting to see him like this," said her grandmother. "Don't you think it breaks my heart every day?"

Rebecca had no idea what to say. "I miss him," she said at last.

Her grandmother shook her head. "Not yet," she said. "He's still here. Under all that disguise, he's still here. He may not be dancing or singing Christmas carols or putting the angel on top of the tree. But I think he's still here, inside there somewhere, in that machine that let him down. He's there."

Rebecca stared at the bed with the person she did not know lying in it.

"Come," said her grandmother after a moment, "let's let him sleep."

Dinner on Christmas Eve was a family tradition. There was turkey, of course, and there would be plum pudding for dessert. Rebecca's father carried in a load of firewood and the logs glowed with good cheer. After dinner there would be carols, an especially rousing rendition of "Joy to the World," and a group recitation of the

shepherds' Christmas story from the book of Luke before each person opened one gift from under the tree.

But this Christmas Eve dinner would be different from all the others.

"Rebecca?" her grandmother called from the kitchen just as the plates of food were being carried to the table. "Rebecca, I need your help."

She hurried to the kitchen with her hands out to accept a bowl of green beans. But she was handed a plate instead.

"I need your help," her grandmother repeated, looking her in the eyes as she placed the plate in her hands. "I'll be busy out here with the turkey for a few more minutes, but I've carved off a few pieces and cut them up and added a little bit of the vegetables. I doubt your grandfather will eat much. But do the best you can."

He was awake this time.

When Rebecca peeked around the corner, she saw the crumpled shape sitting up in bed. She thought again of him as a picture, as a shape, as someone she had never known. Then she took Christmas Eve dinner to her grandfather.

She sat on a stool near his right hand, placing the plate on the tray and, imitating her mother feeding Jeffrey, offered a morsel of food to his mouth.

He wouldn't open it.

Rebecca stared at the small piece of turkey on the fork. She held it half an inch from his mouth but his lips remained tightened. She tried touching it against the skin, but got no response.

Then she felt his hand on her left wrist. She held the fork in her right hand, still offering the food he would not take. His grip held firm to her other hand, so firmly she was surprised by his strength.

And then his hand lifted her hand up. It lifted her hand up to her face. And it brought

With a grip that was firm but never threatening, he held her hand to his face, touching near his own right eye.

the tips of her fingers right up next to her left eye, tapping her head gently.

Then it brought her fingers, and with them her attention, across her lap, across the stainless steel rail, and across the sheets to his own face. With a grip that was firm but never threatening, he held her

hand to his face, touching near his own right eye.

And their eyes met.

It was an embrace. It was a dance. It was an outburst of inappropriate laughter. It was a song. It was an old story retold. It was a walk through the grove on the old path through the snow.

And Rebecca saw him. Maybe for the first time.

She saw him, a fraction of himself but still himself, peeking out from under the burden that had been placed upon him. He was no longer a stranger or a picture or a crumpled pile of sheets.

"Merry Christmas," she said in the softest voice she had ever heard.

"Merry Christmas."

His eyes smiled. He opened his mouth. And he took a bite of turkey. He cleaned his plate that night and again the next morning, when Rebecca was there to wish him a merry Christmas. 🦎

A Christmas Tea

LEE SVITAK DEAN

cup of tea. It may as well be called a cup of cheer, for that is the effect when it is sipped and savored.

The British have a name for their traditional pause in the day, *teatime*. Teatime— part tea, part goodies to nibble—offers refreshment and sustenance for the spirit, as well as for the body. In part that may reflect teatime's importance as a cross between mealtime and entertainment. Whether it's a gathering of family members, children, colleagues, or friends, a pot of tea is not only meant to be sipped, it is meant to be shared.

Europeans drank tea long before the British. Not until Charles II married a Portuguese princess (who brought with her a dowry that included tea) did the beverage find a following in Britain. But Anna, the Duchess of Bedford in the mid-1800s, is credited with creating teatime. Hungry in mid-afternoon with a long wait until dinner, the duchess had tea and treats brought to her room. Others took notice, and by the late nineteenth century, teatime had become a tradition.

Like all traditions, ritual makes up much of this occasion. The British look askance at the American habit of reaching for a tea bag. Loose tea leaves, which give richer flavor, are preferred. The proper way to brew tea, British style, is to begin with fresh water from the tap. It is thought that the flavor will suffer if tea is brewed from water that has sat for a while because then the water has lost its oxygen. The water is brought to a boil, then removed from the heat. Too much boiling also will deplete the oxygen and affect the flavor.

To prepare the teapot, a little hot water is poured into it to warm it, then swirled around and discarded. Next, tea leaves are added to the warmed pot, generally at the rate of one teaspoon per cup of water, plus one extra teaspoon, called "one for the pot." The tea leaves may be put in a metal tea infuser, which can be removed from the pot after the tea has steeped. The tea should steep for three to five minutes. Because the color of tea will vary depending on the type of leaves used, color itself is not a good indicator that the drink is ready.

The tea is served along with a pot of hot water for diluting too-strong cups of tea. Milk or cream, sugar, and lemon are also served alongside, all in pretty dishes. A tea cozy helps to keep the pot hot while the guests are busy nibbling.

The food, and the tea, served traditionally vary by time of day in Britain. The mid-morning equivalent of the American coffee break is *elevens*, the most simple of teatimes, usually limited to tea and a scone or pastry.

Afternoon tea, or *low tea* as it is sometimes called, is served in mid-afternoon, and is probably what most Americans think of when they hear the phrase *teatime*. An abundance of dainty sandwiches and pastries, tarts and cookies are the usual accompaniments to a pot of tea.

Children have *nursery teas* made up of sweets and childlike foods such as puddings, mashed banana sandwiches, and sweet biscuits. Their tea is served diluted with milk.

High tea is the heartiest teatime, often substituting for the evening meal. Although it originated with farm families, high tea is popular in many parts of England. Whereas sweets are the main feature of most other teatimes, high tea is much more of a meal and features many savories, including meats. When served for company, high tea is similar to an hors d'oeuvre buffet.

For a Christmas event, high tea would make for a festive celebration when served in the early evening or for a mid- to late-afternoon party. This is the time to bring out the finest linens, to polish the silver, and to dust off the most delicate bone china. A proper British tea is just that—very proper, with an emphasis on formality.

A menu for just such a holiday high tea follows. It incorporates traditional British tea foods adapted to American tastes. The tea to complement this Christmas menu is Darjeeling, a fragrant Indian tea with a flowery bouquet and rich color that many consider the champagne of teas.

So this Christmas season brew up a pot (or two) of tea to share, and borrow the traditions of the British for a memorable holiday event. ❧

MENU FOR A CHRISTMAS TEA

Mushroom Tarts ❧ Scones with Smoked Turkey or Ham
Scotch Eggs ❧ Potted Shrimp ❧ Chocolate Marmalade Cake ❧ Brandy Snaps

BRANDY SNAPS

Brandy snaps are an ancient cookie served as early as the twelfth century according to some records. They often are part of teatime celebrations. This version adds flavored whipped cream for a wonderful effect.

10½ tbsp. unsalted butter
⅔ cup light corn syrup
¼ cup firmly packed light-brown sugar
1¼ tsp. ground ginger
Pinch of salt
1 cup bleached all-purpose flour
4 tsp. brandy (or imitation brandy-flavored extract)
Whipped Cream Filling

Preheat oven to 350°. In a heavy saucepan, combine butter, corn syrup, sugar, ginger, and salt. Bring the mixture to a boil, stirring often.

Remove from heat and whisk in the flour and brandy. Keep the batter warm and fluid by setting the container in a pan of hot water.

Drop batter by the tablespoon onto two nonstick or greased cookie sheets. They will spread to about 4 inches, so bake only 4 at a time per sheet.

Bake 7 to 10 minutes or until the cookies are a deep golden brown. For even baking, rotate the cookie sheets from top to bottom and front to back halfway through the baking time.

Allow cookies to cool on sheets for about 1 minute or until they can be lifted with a spatula without wrinkling, but are still flexible.

Roll each cookie tightly around a ½ to 1-inch dowel (such as a clean broom handle, cannoli mold, or krumkake mold), pressing down firmly on the seam for a few moments. After it is rolled, place each cookie seam side down on a wire rack to cool. If cookies become too rigid to roll, return them briefly to the oven.

Repeat with remaining batter. It is not necessary to cool the cookie sheets between batches. Store cookies in airtight container at room temperature for up to one week.

Brandy snaps can be filled with whipped cream up to 2 hours ahead if refrigerated, or 1 hour ahead at room temperature. The cream can be whipped several hours ahead, refrigerated and lightly beaten again before using.

Spoon whipped cream into pastry bag. (To create a makeshift pastry bag, use a recloseable gallon-size freezer bag that has been fitted in one corner with a pastry tip, available at most grocery stores.) Pipe whipped cream into the cookies.

Makes 2 dozen cookies.

WHIPPED CREAM FILLING

2 cups heavy cream
1 tbsp. sugar
2 tsp. brandy, if desired
1 tsp. vanilla extract

In large mixing bowl, place heavy cream, sugar, brandy, and vanilla extract; refrigerate for at least 15 minutes, along with the beater.

Beat mixture until stiff peaks form when the beater is raised. Refrigerate until ready to use.

MUSHROOM TARTS

Presentation is a key element of a British tea. Food is generally served in interesting shapes and bite-size portions. These mushroom tarts can be made ahead of time and frozen.

3 oz. cream cheese, softened
½ cup butter or margarine, softened
1 cup flour
¼ tsp. salt
2 tbsp. vegetable oil
¼ cup butter
½ lb. mushrooms, finely chopped
¼ cup parsley, finely chopped
2 tbsp. green onions, finely chopped
   (include some of green tops)
¼ tsp. salt
⅛ tsp. freshly ground pepper
1½ tsp. minced fresh marjoram
   or 1 tsp. crushed dried marjoram
½ cup freshly grated Parmesan cheese
⅓ cup dry bread crumbs

Mix cream cheese and butter together. Add flour and salt; mix well. Chill dough 1 hour. Divide dough into 24 (1-inch) balls. Place balls in miniature muffin tins or in tiny tart pans, pressing dough into sides and bottom of pan (or shape into small crusts by hand). Cover and chill while preparing filling.

In a large skillet heat oil and butter. Sauté mushrooms, parsley, and green onions for 5 minutes, stirring constantly.

Remove from heat and add salt, pepper, marjoram, cheese, and bread crumbs. Mix thoroughly, then allow to cool for 1 hour

Fill unbaked tart shells. (Tarts may be frozen at this point. Cover with plastic wrap and then aluminum foil and freeze unbaked.) If baking right away, bake in preheated oven at 350° for 15 to 20 minutes. (Filling will bubble and pastry turn light brown.) To prepare frozen tarts, defrost 1 hour at room temperature, then bake in preheated oven at 350° for 20 to 25 minutes. Makes 24 miniature tarts.

POTTED SHRIMP

Potting was a method of preserving meat before the days of refrigeration. This version of a British favorite can be prepared in advance and frozen.

½ lb. large uncooked shrimp
2 cloves garlic, minced
½ cup dry sherry
6 tbsp. (¾ stick) butter or margarine
Salt and ground white pepper to taste
1 tbsp. butter or margarine

Peel and devein the shrimp. Combine shrimp, garlic, sherry, and 6 tablespoons butter in a small saucepan and cook over high heat until the shrimp are cooked, about 5 minutes. (If you prefer to save time and use cooked shrimp, cook only garlic, sherry, and butter together instead.)

Add the salt and white pepper to the shrimp mixture. Transfer the mixture to a food processor or blender and purée. Scrape the purée into a ceramic or earthenware pot and refrigerate until set, about 2 hours. Seal the mixture by pouring 1 tablespoon melted butter over the surface. (It will keep like this for 1 week in the refrigerator.) Serve well chilled with crackers, stuffed into cherry tomatoes, or spread on thick slices of cucumber.

To freeze, place in a plastic container and seal the surface with melted butter. Cover tightly and freeze for up to 3 months. Defrost in the refrigerator.

Makes about 1 cup.

CHOCOLATE MARMALADE CAKE

Sweets are an inherent part of any teatime. This chocolate cake, with overtones of orange marmalade, is typical of what would be offered.

3 oz. unsweetened chocolate
1 cup flour
¼ tsp. baking powder
½ tsp. baking soda
½ tsp. salt
¼ cup unsalted butter, softened
1 cup sugar
1 egg
1 cup buttermilk, at room temperature
½ tsp. vanilla extract
½ cup orange marmalade
    (preferably imported bitter style)
Marmalade Glaze

Preheat oven to 350°.
Grease sides of 9-inch springform pan with butter and line bottom with buttered parchment paper. Flour paper and sides of pan; set aside.

Melt chocolate in microwave or in double boiler over hot, but not simmering water, stirring until chocolate melts. Remove from heat and allow to cool to room temperature.

Sift flour, baking powder, baking soda, and salt together. In a separate bowl, cream butter until light; add sugar gradually, beating until mixture is light and fluffy. Add egg and beat thoroughly.

Stir cooled chocolate, vanilla, buttermilk, and marmalade into butter mixture. Gradually add flour mixture until thoroughly combined.

Turn batter into prepared pan. Bake 30 minutes until wooden pick inserted in center of cake comes out clean. Cool cake in pan 10 minutes. Turn out onto wire rack and cool completely.

Poke holes in top of cake with a toothpick. Brush cake with warm Marmalade Glaze (below). Allow glaze to set about 20 minutes before serving.

Serves 10 to 12.

MARMALADE GLAZE
    ¼ cup marmalade
    2 tbsp. orange-flavored liqueur, brandy, or orange juice

In a small saucepan, melt marmalade; blend in liqueur, brandy, or orange juice.

SCOTCH EGGS

Scotch eggs are another traditional British tidbit. Simple to prepare, they are a wonderful savory. Although the recipe must be prepared within 2 hours of baking, if the eggs are hard-cooked in advance, they need only a few minutes more to prepare for the oven.

1 raw egg
1½ lb. ground sausage
Fine bread crumbs
6 hard-cooked eggs, peeled

With hands, mix raw egg into sausage. Divide mixture into six equal portions and mold sausage mixture around hard-cooked eggs. Roll each egg in bread crumbs until well-coated. (Eggs can be prepared up to 2 hours in advance and refrigerated until time to bake.)

Place on a rack in a jelly roll pan and bake at 375° for 45 to 60 minutes, or until sausage is well done. (The rack allows the fat from the sausage to drain off.) Slice each egg into 3 or 4 pieces. Serve at any temperature with a spicy mustard.

Makes 18 to 24 appetizers.

SCONES WITH SMOKED TURKEY OR HAM

Scones are the quintessential British tea food. They come in a variety of shapes (triangles, rounds, squares, and diamonds are most common) and have slight variations in flavor. These sweet scones are served with either ham, a traditional high tea food, or smoked turkey.

2½ cups all-purpose flour
1 tbsp. baking powder
½ tsp. salt
8 tbsp. (1 stick) cold unsalted butter, cut up
⅛ cup granulated sugar
⅔ cup milk
½ to ¾ lb. smoked turkey or thinly sliced ham
Cranberry sauce or fruit chutneys, optional

Heat oven to 425°. Place flour, baking powder, and salt in a large bowl and mix well.

Cut in butter using a pastry blender until the mixture resembles fine granules. Add sugar and toss to mix.

Add milk and stir with a fork until a soft dough forms. Form dough into a ball, place on a lightly floured board, and knead 10 to 12 times.

Roll out dough and cut with 2-inch round cutter. Place on ungreased cookie sheet with scones touching each other. Bake 12 minutes or until tops turn medium brown. Cool completely before serving. To cool, place scones on a wire rack and wrap loosely with a linen or cotton dish towel.

Serve scones along with a platter of smoked turkey or ham for guests to make their own bite-size sandwiches. Cranberry sauce or fruit chutneys may be served on the side.

Makes 18 scones.

THE TEA SET

LOIS McALLISTER

IT'S GOOD TO BE HOME, I think, as I pull into my driveway. Then I see the SOLD sign and am reminded that this is no longer home. In a few minutes movers will be here to load boxes and furniture. By tomorrow morning, I'll be gone, too. Only the shades and curtains will be left to hide the emptiness inside.

I've just come from my mother's funeral. As I take off my black hat and dress, I realize I'm a hypocrite. At funerals, black symbolizes sorrow, and whatever this feeling inside me is, it isn't sorrow.

After the funeral I overheard my sister, Joan, talking to my Aunt Elizabeth about me.

"She's wonderful. Look at how she's bearing up." Joan's speech is a mixture of Kentucky nasality and Texas drawl. It's hard to think of her as a hard-nosed prosecuting attorney when I see her dabbing at her tears with a soggy tissue.

"She'll get through this all right. She's strong, always has been."

They wouldn't have believed me if I had told them the truth.

The mover's shout echoes through the empty house as I leave the bathroom, dressed now in jeans and an oversized plaid flannel shirt. Standing outside the screen door is a large man with an air about him that says he wants to get on with the job to be done. He's scowling at the boxes covering the living room floor, each labelled with my name—Liz Marlow—its contents, and the destination—Colorado Springs, Colorado.

Lifting and tugging, the mover becomes more amenable. "Moving to Colorado, are you? New job?" He pauses to wipe the sweat from his brow with a large red bandanna, which until now has hung from the back pocket of his denim overalls.

"New husband," I answer quickly, to distract myself from the memories provoked by the red bandanna.

"Ah!" A knowing gleam lights up the mover's stubbled face. He makes a quick assessment of me and sees a small woman, thirty-five years old, dressed in work clothes that conceal her shape. Her hair is mussed because she has just removed a black hat and forgot to comb her hair. But he doesn't know about the hat.

"Mr. Marlow in the Air Force?"

I suppose that "Colorado Springs" is the clue. "Yes, the Air Force."

"Pilot?"

"Yes, he's a pilot. Would you like a glass of iced tea?" I look at both him and his helper, a small, silent man standing on the deck just outside the door.

"Yes, ma'am," the helper says with a grin, at last breaking his silence.

Soon the workmen are gone, and I'm alone in an empty house. Aunt Elizabeth has gone back to Louisville, and Joan is on her way back to Texas. As soon as she gets home, she'll call me so that we can comfort each other in the sorrow she believes we share. I know I can't talk to her about what I feel, partly because she wouldn't understand, but mostly because I, myself, don't understand the meaning of this hard knot in my stomach. While I'm trying to decide what I'll say to her, the telephone rings.

It can't be her. She won't be home this soon.

It's my husband, Larry, who again apologizes for not being here with me during what he calls my "difficult time."

"Really, Larry, it's all right," I assure him, and then respond to his concerns as briefly as possible.

"The funeral was beautiful. Reverend James was very kind."

"Yes, the loading was finished without any problems."

"As soon as it's daylight. About 6:30."

"Yes, I'll remember to check the closets and cabinets one more time before I leave."

"Yes, I'm *fine*." I'm surprised at the anger in my voice, and I'm sorry Larry has been on the receiving end of it. I want to talk to him about how I feel, but I can't, any more than I could talk to Joan. I apologize to him and make an excuse about being tired.

"I miss you, too, honey."

After I hang up the phone, I remember that I haven't eaten since breakfast and decide to get a hamburger at a drive-thru window to avoid running into anyone I know. I've already said good-bye and accepted condolences that made me feel awkward and uncomfortable.

I've decided I don't like being a hypocrite.

Later, recalling my promise to Larry, I go to check the closets and cabinets to be sure I haven't missed anything.

The kitchen and bathroom cabinets are clean.

On the floor of a closet in my bedroom I find a receipt for the clothes I bought for my mother's funeral. I wad it up and stuff it into a pocket of my jeans.

In the bedroom my mother used until two weeks ago when she entered the hospital I have to stand on a suitcase to reach the farthest corner of the closet shelf. My hand touches a box, and I hear the tinkle of glass. Carefully, I climb down off the suitcase and set the box on the floor. It's wrapped in brown paper, and written across the front in my mother's distinct handwriting, before arthritis twisted and stiffened her fingers, are the words "For Liz."

Under the brown wrapping is a box covered in cellophane with a note taped to it. Lifting the tape carefully I unfold the small white sheet and read: "Congratulations on your 21st birthday. I know you're a woman now, but this is to let you know you'll always be my baby. Love from Mama." The box contains a toy china set, which is complete, right down to the tiny top for the sugar bowl.

The years fall away, to a hot summer day during my eighth year. I'm sitting on a branch near the top of a tall oak tree in the yard of the house where I was born. On a branch below me are the knots of a rope which holds a board swing. Daddy put the swing there two summers ago, the summer before he died.

"Elizabeth Jane!"

I'm thinking about how much I miss Daddy, and at first I don't pay attention to Mama calling. When she calls again, her voice is louder and more irritated.

She can't see me up here.

The ground looks a long way down, but I know I have to get out of the tree in a hurry.

Mama's mad. If she sees me in the tree, she'll be even madder. What have I done this time?

Tears start to form, and with an effort that takes my breath away, I squeeze my eyes hard to keep them from spilling over.

The impact when I hit the ground jars breath back into my lungs, and I'm so thankful that Mama hasn't seen me in the tree that I don't notice the scrape on my knee from the tree bark. She's coming around the corner of the house with a bucket in her hand.

"I *told* you to get me some water!"

"Yes, Mama." I take the bucket and start for the well.

"What's that on your knee?" Blood is running in a little trickle down my leg.

"You've been up in that tree again. I warned you about that. You know I don't have money to pay for broken arms and legs. Why can't you be good?" She turns away from me and marches toward the kitchen door.

The pulley on the well creaks as I let the well bucket down slowly. When it's filled, I feel the tug of its weight and pull hard, one hand over the other, afraid the rope will slip and I will lose the bucket.

Please don't let me do something else to make Mama mad.

The tears are still there inside me, but I'm determined not to cry.

When the bucket appears at the top of the well, I hold the rope as tightly as I can. It burns as the weight of the water squeezes my fingers.

I pour the water into the bucket Mama has given me, then struggle with my load toward the house. Mama is standing in the kitchen door waiting for me. Her face is set in a dark frown, and she is looking at the bucket instead of me. Without speaking, she takes it from my hand.

I can't hold back the tears any longer. They spill and run down my cheeks.

"I'm sorry, Mama. I won't get up in the tree again. I promise."

Still silent, she turns away from me and takes the water into the kitchen.

Joan, who's twelve, is standing in the door leading from the kitchen to the parlor. She looks at me, then runs out the front door to the veranda, and soon the chains creak in complaint as she pushes herself hard back and forth in the porch swing.

Sitting in a chair at the kitchen table, I bury my face in my folded arms, which are resting on the faded gingham tablecloth. Now my tears become sobs.

"Stop crying," Mama snaps peevishly. "Don't be such a baby."

But I can't stop the choking sounds, even though my throat aches with trying to hold them back. I taste the salt of my tears and wipe them away with the back of my hand. Finally, the lump in my throat dissolves, and my sobs become hiccups that punctuate the hiss of a pressure cooker on the kitchen stove where Mama is canning jars of green beans. Through the blur of tears I look at her, hoping for some sign of sympathy and forgiveness. The scrape on my knee, forgotten until now in the larger pain of knowing Mama is mad at me, begins to throb.

If Daddy were here he would kiss it and make it well. And the flow of tears begins again.

With a metal handle, Mama lifts a cast-iron cover from the top of the big black stove to put a stick of wood inside. First she pokes the fire with the stick to make it burn hotter. The kitchen is already stifling, and she mops the sweat from her forehead with a corner of her apron.

Please wipe my tears and hold me in your lap. Although the words are unspoken, surely she can hear my plea.

But, busy with the canning, Mama has already forgotten me.

My face wet and swollen, I get up quietly and tiptoe through the parlor and out the front door. Joan pretends not to see me as I pass her on my way to a clearing in the woods behind the barn that has been my secret place for the last two years. There I fling myself face down on the warm grass and sob again.

Daddy, where did you go? Why is Mama so mad all the time?

I weep until there are no more tears and the hurt disappears, leaving me numb inside.

On Christmas Eve my Aunt Elizabeth comes. I'm her namesake and the favorite of her nieces and nephews. I'm glad Joan is outside building a snowman so I can have her all to myself.

"Come here and let me see how much you've grown! Why, Lizzie, you grow like a weed. Must be two or three inches since I was here a few weeks ago."

I snuggle into my aunt's ample lap and enjoy the bliss of her arms around me while she rocks me back and forth.

"Don't be such a baby, Elizabeth."

Mama is holding a dark, rich-looking fruitcake. She has on black rubber boots and my father's old brown mackinaw, which covers most of her faded house-dress. A red bandanna is knotted at the back of her head.

"A big eight-year-old like you. You're too big to be rocked."

"Why, of course, she's not too big to be rocked. She's still a baby. A *growing* baby, but a baby all the same. You going to let us eat some of that fruitcake or you just going to let us look at it?"

"I don't know how good it is."

"Pshaw! You know your fruitcake's the best in the world, Lucy, and don't pretend you don't. Here, I'll cut it."

Aunt Elizabeth hands me a large slice of the fruitcake, which has stood in a dark cupboard wrapped in a cider-soaked cloth for six weeks. The odor is heady to an eight-year-old. I look up at Mama.

"If you get sick, don't blame me." She turns abruptly and goes into the kitchen.

I take the cake and snuggle deeper into Aunt Elizabeth's comforting arms.

> *That night I try to stay awake for Santa Claus. The snow is deep—deep enough to make snow cream from the drifts. Enough for Santa's reindeer and sleigh to get here.*

The kitchen door opens and closes and soon we hear the thwack of an axe on wood.

That night I try to stay awake for Santa Claus. I can hear Joan's steady breathing beside me. The attic room is cold, but the feather bed we sleep on and the patchwork quilt, which Mama has sewn from scraps left over from making our dresses, keeps us warm. I draw the quilt up over my head and wait and listen.

The snow is deep—deep enough to make snow cream from the drifts where the top layer can be brushed away to uncover the clean snow underneath.

Enough for Santa's reindeer and sleigh to get here.

The next thing I know it's Christmas morning, and daylight is coming through the attic window. Quietly, so as not to awaken Joan, I slip out of bed and tiptoe to the window. Standing on a stool, I can look through the window for footprints and sleigh tracks in the snow. Except for

Joan's snowman, the white blanket covering the yard is unmarked.

Santa Claus hasn't come since Daddy died. This is three Christmases.

I shiver as I take off my warm flannel gown and put on my cotton underwear and stockings, my brown wool dress, and my oxford shoes. Joan is still asleep.

I guess she knew Santa Claus wouldn't come.

At the foot of the stairs, I can see into the parlor where the Christmas tree with its garlands of popcorn and paper chains stands. Its branches droop.

Poor Christmas tree.

But under the tree are two packages. I tiptoe over to look at them, and one has a tag with "For Elizabeth" written on it. It's a big box wrapped in green plaid paper printed with red and white striped candy canes and tied with red ribbon. The other package, which is smaller, is for Joan.

My heart pounds.

Then I remember—Santa's reindeer fly through the air and land on the roof. That's why there are no tracks in the snow.

I jump when I hear Mama's voice.

"Go wake up Joan, then come set the table."

After breakfast Joan opens her gift first. She has a red book satchel, and for a minute I'm jealous. But only for a minute. Sitting on the floor, I take the ribbon and paper off my box carefully and lay them aside. With shaky hands I lift the top. Inside is a toy china tea set.

Bright red and blue flowers decorate each delicate piece. The edges of the plates and saucers and the cup handles are trimmed in gold. I hold the cover for the sugar bowl in my palm, and the tiny gold knob on top shines like a gold nugget. I look up to show Mama and see an expression on her face I haven't seen for two years. When my eyes meet hers, the look quickly vanishes and is replaced by the firm lines that have been there since the night of my father's death.

"Take them up to your room and pick up this mess; then come dry the dishes," she says sharply.

"Yes, Mama."

I'm afraid to pick up this big box.

Mama, will you carry it for me? But the words go unspoken. She has left the room, and anyway, she would say I'm big enough to do for myself.

I make it safely to my room with my treasure and leave it there while I help

Joan dry the dishes and carry in the wood Mama cut the day before.

In the evening Aunt Elizabeth returns home from her visit to my uncle on the next farm. She talks with Mama in the parlor while I wait, impatient for her attention.

"Now, how about those dishes you want me to see?" she says finally, and at once I hurry off to get the tea set.

Then carefully, carefully I come down the stairs, each foot placed firmly on the next step down before the other is lifted to continue the descent. Finally I stand in front of Aunt Elizabeth, eager to share the beauty of my treasure.

But my hands are cramped from holding the big box so tightly. It slips from my grasp, and the dishes are broken into little pieces scattered across the linoleum. I fall to my knees and stare in disbelief at the bits of glass which are all that remain of my beautiful china. Even the top with its gold nugget has disappeared among the fragments on the floor.

Which is stronger, my grief at the loss of the first treasure I have ever owned or my dread of the look on Mama's face? The dread vanishes when I glance up at her out of the corner of my eye. Her expression is the same as when I unwrapped the dishes, except now the look of love is followed by a look of sadness that matches my own. I know in that instant that there isn't any Santa Claus.

> *I take the ribbon and paper off my box carefully and lay them aside. With shaky hands I lift the top. Inside is a toy china tea set.*

The dishes were a present from Mama. Aunt Elizabeth goes to get a broom to sweep up, and Mama goes into the kitchen. We never speak of the tea set,

and we never speak of the feelings we shared on that last night of my childhood.

It's nearly dark in the empty house.
I ought to get up and turn on a light.
But the memories are not over. I recognize the salty taste in my mouth.

Scenes from the years after that Christmas form and reform in my mind like the bright pieces of colored glass in a child's kaleidoscope. As a result of seeing my mother struggle to keep Joan and me clothed and fed, I develop independence and a strong determination to be financially secure. Soon Joan is a fledgling attorney, and I'm entering graduate school, set on owning a management consulting business before I reach thirty.

While I'm studying for my graduate school entrance exam, I receive a letter from my mother asking if I can be at

home the following Sunday, which is my twenty-first birthday. I call her and explain about studying for the exam. Our conversation is one between friends, not between mother and daughter. She sounds disappointed that I won't be there, but she doesn't reproach me.

The goal I had set for myself for thirty is reached at twenty-eight. I feel secure enough to buy a house, and Mama comes to live with me. She worries that I've never married and talks about the biological time clock. I remind her that Joan and I were both children of her middle age. When, at last, at age thirty-four, I meet Larry Marlow at a ski resort and fall in love, she is satisfied.

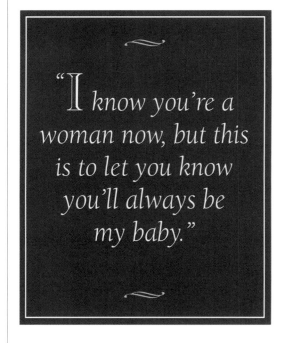

On our wedding day a year later she admires my dress, then pats me on the shoulder and wishes me happiness. I feel a lump in my throat, and as I did when I was little, I close my eyes tightly to hold back the tears. On this most important day of my life, I want to talk about the feelings that have been mute between us since my father's death twenty-nine years ago. But today it's the same as all the times before when I've wanted to talk to her about my feelings. I become a little girl again, trapped in my loneliness and hurt, needing the comfort of her arms around me—more than just a pat on the shoulder. So again, I choke back the sobs that form in my chest and take away my breath. I remind myself that I'm not a baby anymore and tell her that Larry and I will spend the next two weeks getting the new house ready and then I will be back to get her for the move to Colorado Springs.

But when I return, my mother is in the hospital with Aunt Elizabeth standing over her bed looking anxious. Within a week, she is dead.

I read the words on the note again. "I know you're a woman now, but this is to let you know you'll always be my baby." Then I take the tiny top of the sugar bowl out of the box. The knob shines like a gold nugget. With my hand closed around it tightly, I feel the hard knot in my stomach disappear. In its place is a feeling that at last I can recognize.

> "I know you're a woman now, but this is to let you know you'll always be my baby."

The telephone is ringing again. Wiping my eyes with the back of my hand, I put the top back into the box, then struggle to my feet. Slowly I grope my way along the dark hall to the phone in the living room.

"Yes, Larry, I've been crying."

Again I'm sorry for him. I know he wants to comfort me, but just as I couldn't talk to him about my anger this morning, I can't talk to him about my sorrow. I tell him I'll be all right and not to worry.

After I say good-bye, I put the phone in its holder on the wall and switch on the ceiling light. I glance at my watch.

It's probably still too early, but I think I'll try to call Joan anyway.

I reach into my pocket for a tissue but find only the crumpled receipt for the black hat and dress. I wipe the fresh flow of tears from my eyes with the corner of my flannel shirt as I reach for the telephone and dial the number in Dallas.

THE TWELVE DAYS OF CHRISTMAS

On the first day of Christmas
my true love sent to me
A partridge in a pear tree.

On the second day of Christmas
my true love sent to me
Two turtle doves, . . .

On the third day of Christmas
my true love sent to me
Three french hens, . . .

On the fourth day of Christmas
my true love sent to me
Four calling birds, . . .

On the fifth day of Christmas
my true love sent to me
Five gold rings, . . .

On the sixth day of Christmas
my true love sent to me
Six geese a-laying, . . .

On the seventh day of Christmas
my true love sent to me
Seven swans a-swimming, . . .

On the eighth day of Christmas
my true love sent to me
Eight maids a-milking, . . .

On the ninth day of Christmas
my true love sent to me
Nine ladies dancing, . . .

On the tenth day of Christmas
my true love sent to me
Ten lords a-leaping, . . .

On the eleventh day of Christmas
my true love sent to me
Eleven pipers piping, . . .

On the twelfth day of Christmas
my true love sent to me
Twelve drummers drumming, . . .

Our Christmas
~

Christmas Eve
_____
_____
_____
_____

Christmas Day
_____
_____
_____
_____

Christmas Worship
_____
_____

Christmas Guests
_____
_____
_____
_____
_____

Christmas Gifts
_____
_____
_____
_____
_____

ISBN 0-8066-8980-3

Augsburg Fortress
17-144